WABI SABI
侘 寂

Learning the ancient japanese art of imperfection with thoughtfulness and peacefulness.
Conceptual art and Minimalism

© Copyright 2019 by Hinata Kobayashi

All rights reserved.

Table of Contents

DISCLAIMER 10
© Copyright 2019 by Hinata Kobayashi 11
INTRODUCTION 13
HISTORY OF WABI SABI 16
CHAPTER ONE 27
  Origins of wabi sabi 27
    Murata Juko and his letter from the heart 31
    Charatcetistics of wabi sabi 34
    The relevance of wabi-sabi in the past 48
    The relevance of wabi-sabi today 55
    What is / not is wabi sabi 59
CHAPTER TWO 74
  Culture 74
    What does "Japanese feel of flaw" truly mean? 76
    Japanese Character 79
    The monkey doesn't know 83
CHAPTER THREE 88
  Living with Nature 88
    What exactly are kintsugi and wabi-sabi? 88
    Take into account your shortcoming 89

Hold the Resistor. 89

Become a better version of yourself. 89

Practice self-esteem and forgiveness.............. 90

Japanese aesthetic philosophy offers a new perspective on the so-called about our physical errors. 91

Exceeding perfection 93

Enjoy the process 94

Accept the change 95

How to live in a wabi-sabi style and embrace imperfection 95

How to accept your lack 96

So what is the wabi-sabi lifestyle?................... 96

Find the tribe on social media 97

Get inspired by nature...................................... 98

How to Follow the Wabi-Sabi Lifestyle 99

How wabi-sabi can improve your well-being.. 100

Five principles live in a wabi-sabi style 101

The beauty of imperfection............................. 101

What is Wabi-Sabi? 102

Wabi-Sabi makes us happier 103

Wabi-Sabi is the interior: nature and simplicity 104

Wabi-Sabi inside in six stages....................... 104

Wabi-Sabi is not just about accepting imperfection 106

How does wabi-sabi fit into regular culture in these different places? 107

What are the best tips to incorporate wabi-sabi into our day by day lives? 110

Wabi-sabi's character is human 111

What have the empty trays to do with interrupting my inner critic? 112

Moral precept of wabisabi 115

Wabi-sabi/ Myer Fabry 118

What is wabi-sabi, and for what reason is it hard to characterise? 119

How is wabi-sabi different from modernism? How is it the same? 120

What is the metaphysical basis of wabi-sabi? What are its spiritual values? 120

What is the wabi-sabi state of mind? What are its moral precepts? 121

What are the material qualities of wabi-sabi? 121

CHAPTER FOUR 123

Wabi-sabi Simplifying 123

How does Wabi-Sabi improve simplification? 124

The terms are combined for the sake of simplicity. 125

An Ancient philosophical term 126

Here are some ways to change your mind with wabi-sab: 130

He would be a fool to haunt perfection and its short forms. 134

wabi-sab's philosophy has captured the interior world with natural wood furniture and bowls .. 134

Which means wabi-sabi 135

Wabi-Sabi and Thoughtfulness 136

Worn Interiors and Trouser Bowls 137

How you have a Home and a Loved One 138

Wabi-Sabi-Way 139

Invest in Wabi-sabi ideale for your own home and style 140

CHAPTER FIVE 144

Spiritual 144

Metaphysical basis 145

Demystifying Wabi-Sabi 145

Definition 146

Hiding certain movements 150

The Wabi-Sabi universe 151

Metaphysical Foundations 151

Spiritual value 152

The truth comes from observing nature 153

- CHAPTER SIX 156
  - Soul Nurturing 156
    - A new way 157
    - How to inspire touch shopping 159
    - Principles for wabi-sab 160
    - Ways to build flexibility 163
    - Questions to help you adapt to nature 164
    - See the beauty in imperfection 166
- CHAPTER SEVEN 169
  - State of Mind 169
    - State of Mind Guide 171
    - Around without flowers in bloom 172
    - Material quality 173
    - Similarities 175
    - Beauty is Empty 177
    - What are the doctrines of the universe? 177
    - Highlights 178
    - Wabi-Sabi to everyone 182
    - What is the metaphysical basis of wabi-sab? What are your spiritual values? 183
    - What is the Wabi-Sabi state of mind? What are your moral rules? 184
    - What are the material properties of wabi-sab? 184

- Japanese aesthetics standard and simplicity 185
- What is wabi-sabi, and for what reason is it hard to characterise? 186
- The beauty of wabi sabi 188
- And by focusing more on what remains. 194

CHAPTER EIGHT 196

Design 196
- Wabi-Sabi-design? 196
- Let Wabi-Sabin look at home 196

Principles in design 197
- Use natural materials 198
- Keep it simple 198
- Take on the flaws 199

The Wabi-Sabi Materials 200
- Accepting Home History 201
- Make corrections with a gold leaf 201
- Antiques and antique furniture 201
- Fixed elements 201
- Incomplete art 202
- Concrete floors 202
- Handmade objects 202
- Antique Mirrors 202
- Natural materials 203

Textured walls 203
CHAPTER NINE 205
　Wabi-Sabi Art 205
　　Place the Wabi-Sabi-tie 205
　　My philosophy on Wabi-Sabi art 207
　　We appreciate where we are and enjoy the trip 208
　　Developing the Wabi-Sabi spirit 209
　　The art of imperfection 210

DISCLAIMER

All intellect contained in this book is given for enlightening and instructive purposes as it were. The creator isn't in any capacity responsible for any outcomes or results that radiate from utilising this material. Worthwhile endeavours have been made to give data that is both precise and viable. However, the creator isn't oriented for the exactness or use/misuse of this data.

© Copyright 2019 by Hinata Kobayashi

All rights reserved.

This document is geared towards providing exact and reliable information with regard to the topic and issue covered. The publication is sold with the idea that the publisher is not required to render accounting, officially permitted, or otherwise qualified services. If advice is necessary, legal or professional, a practised individual in the profession should be ordered.

From a Declaration of Principles which was accepted and approved equally by a Committee of the American Bar Association and a Committee of Publishers and Associations.

In no way is it legal to reproduce, duplicate, or transmit any part of this document in either electronic means or printed format. Recording of this publication is strictly prohibited, and any storage of this document is not allowed unless with written permission from the publisher. All rights reserved.

The information provided herein is stated to be truthful and consistent, in that any liability, in terms of inattention or otherwise, by any usage or abuse of any policies, processes, or directions contained within is the sole and utter responsibility of the recipient reader. Under no circumstances will any legal liability or blame be held against the publisher for any reparation, damages, or monetary loss due to the information herein, either directly or indirectly.

Respective authors own all copyrights not held by the publisher.

The information herein is offered for informational purposes solely and is universal as so. The presentation of the data is without a contract or any guarantee assurance.

The trademarks that are used are without any consent, and the publication of the trademark is without permission or backing by the trademark owner. All trademarks and brands within this book are for clarifying purposes only and are owned by the owners themselves, not affiliated with this document.

INTRODUCTION

Japanese cultural standards and definitions of beauty were feeding for generations. Since the Heian era, Japan has revived its focus on the natural world by embracing its unpredictable nature.

Fluctuations and acceptance of sensitivity and respect for life. The Japanese have developed a distinctive aesthetic feeling, including wabi-sabi, a monkey they are unaware of and able to channel their attitudes towards nature and its impact on art and culture. Each of these aesthetics represents a different kind of beauty, often portraying the beauty of unexpected forms. Wabi-Sabi represents rustic and deserted beauty; unconscious monkey, fast and versatile beauty; Oh, empty or reckless beauty.

In defining visions through this aesthetic presentation, Japan has it created awareness of the beauty of nature that is not usually found other societies, especially after fragmentation. It's Japan It has always been a vision-focused nation in all areas of culture: you arts such as poetry and calligraphy; through rituals like ancient tea ceremony; and consumer goods in contemporary urban life in Japan and architecture. The

Japanese have a good view of their surroundings skilfully blended classical aesthetics with modern development, referring to its natural emphasis on the root Reduce his eternal presence in society. For example, Kyoto The station is a central feature of Kyoto's cityscape, central Kyoto. downtown and its modern architecture demonstrates features that characteriseCharacterise the cities of Japan. Although there has been an exhibition at Kyoto Station recently innovation in synthetic size still contains elements The simplicity of design and continuity with nature.

The development has extended the coverage to the Kyoto base however, there are numerous temples and gardens on the hillsides. Amid his communal areas, he continues to show Japanese awareness of his relationship with nature. The surrounding environment. these human-made temple spaces reinforce their unnaturalness features: without character, they would be cold, supernatural buildings that are isolated from the environment. These are the changing elements nature adds to the emotions and feelings that a person has in response to artificial creations among nature's existence, as human beings should continuously aware of their place in life. Japanese awareness of this increases gratitude for these traditions and Natural elements of modern society. Although sometimes tricky to recognise, the integration of life into the industrialised, industrialised world Community is an essential part of beauty for success in development Strong modern culture. Without this integration, the character is created to counter human progress by provoking constant resistance understanding the origin of both domains that aesthetic and their role in ancient Japanese culture, and one can understand why they still have a significant impact Current Urban Japan.

HISTORY OF WABI SABI

Wabi-Sabi (侘 寂) Presents a complete or aesthetic picture of the Japanese world, focusing on the transition and imperfection. Aesthetics is sometimes described as beauty which is "imperfect, permanent and imperfect". It is a conception derived from the Buddhist teaching of the three aspects of existence (印 印 sanbōin), In particular of immutability (無常 mujō), Two other suffering (苦 Ku) And the emptiness or lack of nature (三法 kū).

Wabi-Sabi aesthetics are characterised by asymmetry, unevenness (unevenness or irregularity), simplicity, economy, frugality, modesty, closeness, and the evaluation of the naive integrity of natural objects and processes.

"Wabi-Sabi is the most striking and characteristic feature of traditional Japanese beauty, and it has roughly the same position in the pantheon of Japanese aesthetic values as the Greek ideals of beauty and perfection in the West." If an object or expression can arouse in us a sense of peaceful melancholy and spiritual longing, that object can be said to be Wabi-Sab. [Wabi-Sabi] cherishes all genuine by recognising three simple realities: nothing lasts, nothing is complete, and nothing is perfect. "

Wabi and Sabi are challenging to decipher. Wabi initially alluded to the depression of living in nature, far from society; Sabi means "cold", "thin" or "drained". Around the fourteenth century, these meanings began to change and became more positive connotations. [1] Wabi now stands for rustic simplicity, freshness or tranquillity, and can be used in natural and artificial objects or subtle elegance. It can also refer to the peculiarities and abnormalities of the building process that add uniqueness and style to the purpose. Sabi is beauty or serenity that is associated with years in which the lifetime and durability of an object are demonstrated by its patina and wear or any visible repair.

After conquering artistic and Buddhist influences from China for centuries, the wabi-sab eventually became an unmistakably Japanese perfect. After some time, the implications of wabi and sabi have become cheerful and hopeful. About 700 years ago, especially among Japanese nobility, the understanding of emptiness and imperfection was valued as the first step toward a tent or enlightenment. In today's Japan, the meaning of wabi-sab is often condensed to "the wisdom of natural simplicity." Artbooks generally define it as "imperfect beauty".

From a design or design point of view, wabi can be interpreted as an imperfect quality of any product due to inevitable design and construction/manufacturing limitations, especially given the unpredictable or changing operating conditions; I knew then that this could be interpreted in terms of the imperfect reliability or limited mortality of any object, resulting in a phonological and etymological connection with the Japanese word Sabi to be oxidised. Namely, although in addition to the Japanese kanji characters 錆 (Sabi meaning "rust") and 寂 (Sabi as above), and their applied meanings, the original spoken word (pre-kanji, Yamato-Kotoba) is believed to be the same.

    A great example of this embodiment can be seen in the individual styles of Japanese ceramics. Ceramic items used in the Japanese tea ceremony were often rustic and dull in appearance, such as Hague articles, whose shapes are not entirely symmetrical, and colours or textures that appear to emphasise a pure or unclean style. Based on the knowledge and observations of the participant, hidden signs of truly magnificent design or enamel (similar to the appearance of a rough diamond) can be detected and detected. This can be interpreted as a kind of Wabi-Sabi aesthetic, which further reinforces the knowledge that enamelled articles change colour over time as water is repeatedly poured into them (Sabi) and the fact that teapots are often intentionally broken or cut. (wabi), which acts as a signature of the Hagi-Yaki style.

    Both Wabi and Sabi refer to feelings of desertion and loneliness. In the Mahayana Buddhist vision of the universe, these can be considered as positive features that represent the liberation and transcendence of the material world towards a simpler life. However, the Mahayana philosophy warns that genuine understanding cannot be achieved through words or language, so accepting wabi-sab in non-verbal circumstances might be the most appropriate approach. Simon Brown points out that Wabi-Sabi describes how students can learn to live the life of the senses and participate in life better than they do, rather than worrying about unnecessary thoughts. In this sense, Wabi-Sabi is a material account of Zen Buddhism. The thought is that being encompassed by normal, changing and unique objects helps us connect with the real world and avoid potentially stressful distractions.

Wabi-Sabi is, in a sense, a practice through which Wabi-Sabi students learn to find the most basic, natural, enjoyable, fascinating, and beautiful objects. Faded pre-winter leaves would be a model. Wabi-Sabi can change our impression of the world to such an extent that a chip or fracture in a vase makes it exciting and gives the subject a more meditative value. Similarly, ageing materials such as bare wood, paper and fabric become more attractive because they show changes that can be observed over time.

The terms wabi and sabi are initially religious, but the actual use of the word in Japanese is often quite informal. The synchronicity of Japanese belief systems must be emphasised.

When searching for information on the history or origins of wabi-sab, you will almost always find a link to 16th century Japan and the legend of tea teacher Sen no Rikyū. The Japanese worshipped Rikyū and considered him the first person to understand the core of this cultural and philosophical direction. His way to deal with the feel of common effortlessness primarily developed new forms of Japanese architecture, garden design, fine art, and applied technique. But he is not someone who one day decided to create wabi-sabi from scratch.

Buddha

Of course, there can be no exact date when the original wabi-sabi has wholly begun. Wabi-Sabi is based on Zen Buddhism and is its unique expression. For this reason, it is sometimes claimed that supremacy dates back to 563 BC, when Prince Siddhartha Gautama, later known as Buddha, found compassion for human suffering and left the material world. Presently the historical backdrop of Buddhism and Zen Buddhism should proceed. But we'll summarise and jump a few centuries later:

Tea ceremony

Zenit Buddhism's late 13th-century tea ceremony began to spread from China to Japan. In the early 14th century, the art of tea ceremony was also developed in Japan, mostly thanks to Buddhist priests.

Over the next two centuries, the tea ceremony evolved in the most typical way to practice Zen philosophy. But at the same time, in a human form that combines the required skills of architecture, interior design, garden design, flower arrangements, painting, cooking and exhibition. The tea master also had to make sure that current guests were included in the silent artistic event.

Japanese tea retailers recently used teapots in the 16th and early 16th centuries as golf courses around the world. Trade talks, stabilisation and the dissolution of political alliances were negotiated there. It used expensive, richly decorated Chinese ceramic materials. Usually, it was the aesthetics of wealth and exaggerated ornamentation, mainly from China. Tea was considered a form of entertainment for the elite.

Murata Jukō

Murata Jukō By the end of the 16th century, Zenic monk Murata Jukō began to rebel against the current rules of the tea ceremony. For example, opening access to a tea party even for ordinary people. This period of tea ceremony ended with some exaggeration for the elect. He also began to use unobtrusive pottery made daily by local people. This is also the reason why Jukō is mentioned as the first known wabi-sabi theme master.

Sen from Rikyū

One No Rikyū One hundred years later, in the 16th century, we have already achieved the most famous character of wabi-sab: The No Rikyū Master (1522-1591), under which wabi-sabi reached its peak. Its no Rikyū legend is often mentioned, which in its simplicity describes the wabi-sabi principle.

Legend of Sen from Rikyū

Its no Rikyū was a young man who wanted to learn the art of tea function. So he went to the celebrated tea ace Takeno Jōō who told him to clean and burn the leaf garden as an entrance exam. After thorough work, Rikyū checked the garden's full and perfect appearance. Before it showed to his teacher, however, he shook the wood, a Japanese red maple tree and a few beautifully coloured leaves fell to the ground.

According to another version of the story, Sakura blossoms and Rikyū shakes the tree to blow a few flowers. I don't know, but our garden has a Japanese cherry tree. When it blooms, it is beautiful, but the flowers fall without shaking the tree. However, this story is somewhat characterised by the beauty of Wabi-Sabi's incompleteness, temporality and incompleteness.

There is a similar story about how Rikyū, many years later, rebuked his son, a future student of the tea ceremony, for adequately cleaning the garden.

Well, it's a legend, and it sounds a bit deceptive. But it was in the 16th century. A year that was not very beautiful. Not in Asia or Europe. It was a time of steady war and unfeelingness, yet also fruitful art, including Japanese tea ceremonies.

Rikyū, the eldest of the masters.

Rikyū became a thief and one of the best here. His approach to the aesthetics of simplicity developed new forms of Japanese architecture, garden design, visual and applied art.

But back to reality, Japan, the 16th century. Rikyū became known and respected in his life. This worried Hideyoshi, his superior and protector, that he ordered seventy tea masters Rikyuta to commit ritual suicide (Harakiri).

Wabi-sabi-story of Sen no Rikyū

Harmony, respect, purity, and serenity are not only the foundation of tea ceremonies but remain. Even the Japanese worship Rikyu even today, and is considered the first to understand the essence of the artistic and philosophical direction of Wabi-Sabi: the art of finding beauty in imperfection that weighs every moment in its transience, the honour of genuineness. Wabi-Sabi is translated as "the knowledge of common effortlessness".

CHAPTER ONE

Origins of Wabi Sabi

Wabi-Sabi is an old Japanese way of philosophy that spotlights on the defect and transient nature of life. It has its roots in Buddhism and was born of tea ceremonies where precious supplies are handmade, irregular and defective. There is no direct Western translation for Wabi-Sab, but above all, it is the art of finding beauty in the imperfect, the unstable and the imperfect.

Wabi-Sabi house

It is fair to say that in the West, we are obsessed with perfection. But you won't find wabi-sab in a bright new building or perfectly combined furniture. It cannot be purchased.

Wabi-Sabi is an excellent homemade carrot; cracks in the ceramic container; a book that burns well; cherry blossom; a worn wooden corridor and elbow at your favourite bathroom. It is an appreciation of everything pure, humble and incomplete.

Authenticity is a big part of the wabi sab, so cracks and imperfections are nourished to symbolize the progression of time and adoring use. Accepting Wabi-Sab at home teaches us to be content with our current party without the constant need for more. It is the perfect antidote to a discarded society based on disposable and homogeneous mass products.

Adoption of Wabi-Sab

You shouldn't be a specialist in the Japanese way of philosophy or have a large budget to implement the principles of Wabi-Sab at home. There are no "wrong" ways to achieve this; You need to change your perspective from one improvement to another.

The farm may have a kitchen table that has been passed down from one generation to the next. It is well used and displayed with multiple marks and scratches. Instead of being ashamed of his immunity, he should appreciate it for its imperfect nature. These signs of use are stories and signify the passage of time; This significance is not found in the new boxing board.

Of course, sometimes it is necessary to buy new things. Things are changing, kids, coming and going, moving from home, new hobbies, etc. When purchasing, you need to consider the wabi-sabi approach and choose from thousands of used or used items.

Wabi-Sabi means appreciating nature, so pay attention to the materials you bring to your home and look for natural alternatives such as wood and stone wherever possible. They are tastefully satisfying as well as utilitarian. Take linen and, for example, heal every wash.

You can also look for inspiration from nature when choosing colours. This leaves plenty of room for personal choice as the pink colour of the cherry blossom is as natural as a relaxed and relaxing plate. Storm grey is just as natural as pine.

It may be tempting to add new things to your home regularly, but wabi-sabi requires removing unnecessary items to have a good life for yourself. Consider getting rid of unnecessary details by getting rid of the extra clutter. Doing so will empower essential things to stand out and shine.

Additional Services

Wabi-Sabi's acceptance means more than just creating a comfortable home environment. Our love for our homes and imperfect features reduces the need to buy as many new products as possible. It reduces consumption, which saves money and reduces the burden on our planet.

And our opinion is changing. Wabi-Sabi focuses on gratitude for things that already exist, instead of always wanting something new and bright. This mighty change of perspective helps us to feel calmer and happier in the present, and thus enable us to embrace the peace and tranquillity of everyday life.

Outside of homes, wabi-sabi provides a useful framework for modern life in general. Finding beauty in imperfection, appreciating nature, and fighting for joy are not new and bright ideas. Still, it's good to remember them the next time you write on Pinterest's rabbit wishes.

The original Wabi-Sabi seed was derived from sintered Zen Buddhism. Chinese Zen Buddhism focused on the humble reality and the unclean way of life. He accepted the acceptance of uncontrolled nature and humanity and life. These rules took place throughout China and influenced the work of poets and artists as they left. Chinese art was minimalist in the early nineteenth century, expressing an atmosphere of anxiety and melancholy. In the mid-nineteenth century, the suppression of the foreign influence of Tang Emperor Wuzong began. This suppressed Buddhism, as did the ideas of Zoroastrianism and Maniha in China. In spite of Chinese control, the standards of Zen Buddhism have, as of now reached Japan.

These theories became established at the beginning of the Japanese aesthetic philosophy origin of Wabi-Sab. Japanese culture has embedded this philosophy in almost every aspect of it. For the aristocratic class, the Wabi-Sabi apotheosis was a tea ceremony.

Japanese Tea Party

The Japanese Tea Ceremony is a multidisciplinary art form that combines architecture, gardening, painting and presentation with tea drinking. A tea master ceremony can combine these sciences in an idiosyncratic orchestra. An isolated event for guests and the host that demands calm attention and appreciation. An assessment of the moment and its subtle impact on the world. The goal of a tea ceremony practitioner is to confirm such an event. A game that represents the pinnacle of applied wabi-sabi philosophy.

Murata Juko and his letter from the heart

By the fifteenth century, the tea function had become elite entertainment. Demonstrating prosperity and related authority. Displaying your articles on Chinese tea. Items with the right shape and perfect enamel. Murata Juko responded to these elements of the tea ceremony that culminated in his composition Heart Letter. The work was both a discussion of the method and an aesthetic evaluation of the tea service. Juko underscored four components in his tea service; relative, Kei, sei, Ji. Kin, ceremonial piety. Hey, self-respect. Sei, purity of body and spirit. Ji, the liberation of desires and basic impulse. In his tea ceremonies, Juko used Japanese and Chinese instruments to harmonise opposing tastes. Juko has stated that too much aesthetics cannot be tolerated at the tea ceremony; The aesthetic needed to be unified and mixed. The Heart Letter was the first codification of the Wabi-Sabi philosophy.

Tea ceremony interior design elements.

Wabi-Sabi brought it to its peak, in the 16th century, Sen no Rikyu. The son of a Murat Yuk merchant and a disciple, Rikyu started as Oda Nobunaga's theme teacher. After Nobunaga's death, Rikyu took over the work of his successor, Toyotomi Hideyoshi. During this time, Japanese society experienced a transition from medieval to modern times, which influenced Japanese culture. This effect extended to the tea ceremony, which began with intense experimentation and evolution. Each component of the service is analysed: functions, objects, and architecture.

Rikyu understood the implicit emotional content of the tea filling and began to summarise the ceremony. The tea ceremony, which has no unnecessary qualities, has become its present element two mat mats and two vanity cups in a thick mud apartment, a feeling of simplicity. Because Hideyoshi considered offensive to his peasant's origin and jealousy of his growing reputation and property, he ordered ritual suicide to Sen Riki.

Wabi-Sabi modern

Since Rikyu's death, several factions have emerged and competed. Forced by his "true" interpretation of Rikyo's teachings, the imagination of the tea ceremony was almost gone. Each activity and theme is defined. The tea ceremony changed from art to fashion.

The focus of the tea ceremony was shifting away from the fundamental need of Wabi-sab. The repeated actions lost all meaning and thought behind them. Although an object may have aesthetics without the wabi-sabi process, the purpose cannot be considered as a wabi-sabi process.

Several groups interested in reviving the Wabi-Sabi philosophy have invited contemporary artists and designers to bring new ideas to the Tea Party and with it the Wabi-Sabi philosophy. The truth will surface eventually how this methodology will back off.

Charatcetistics of wabi sabi

Wabi and Sabi: Aesthetics of Loneliness

Almost all the arts of historical China and Japan follow their aesthetic principles of Taoism and Zen Buddhism. The two great philosophical traditions proved to be particularly compatible with Japanese culture and psychology. A feature of a Chinese or Japanese masterpiece that has no contemporary influence is still its naturalness and raw appearance, even the "coincidence" of the work. The artist works and harmonises nature and its general disasters. The core values are wabi and sabi.

Wabi

The two prevailing standards of Chinese and Japanese art and culture are Wabi and Sabi. Wabi alludes to a philosophical structure, a sense of space, direction, or path, while Sabi is an aesthetic structure that stems from a particular object and its features, as well as interest in time, chronology and objectivity. Although the terms are and should be spoken, they are generally associated with wabi-Sabina, functional description and a unique aesthetic principle.

The original wabi connotation is based on the loneliness or detachment experienced by hermits in society, which causes misery and sadness in the minds of people. It was distinctly in the fourteenth century that wabi was given positive qualities in Japan and cultivated. As Koren1 says,

The hermit and ascetic self-described isolation and voluntary poverty were seen as opportunities for spiritual prosperity.

Wabi is poverty, but it was not related to the lack of material wealth, but the independence of material wealth. Wabi is the destruction of material that transcends material wealth. Wabi is a simplicity that has blended content with a direct view of nature and reality. This lack of addiction also does not include pampering, decoration and arrogance. Wabi is a quiet delight in simple things.

In short, a wabi is a journey of a life or a spiritual journey. It precedes the application of the aesthetic principles applicable to objects and art, the latter being wise. The Zenic principles, which informed Wabi, enjoyed a vibrant blend of Confucian, Taoist, Buddhist and Shinto traditions, but focused on the hermit vision and the reasons why the hermit began to follow hermitian. These philosophical ideas are known: the recognition of duality as an illusion, the attachment to the ego and the material world of suffering, the fear of death that prevents sexual life, the appreciation of the decency of life as the body lives in harmony with nature.

The hermit life in Japan is called wabizumai, mainly "wab life", a life of loneliness and simplicity.

Although many Japanese characters from the 15th and 16th centuries are distinguished in their transition from wab to sab (Shuko, Rikyu, Ikkyu), the process was already organic between poets and artists. The tea ceremony was Sab's first "artificial" expression, meaning that the principles of wab are incorporated into specific objects and activities.

Sabi

Sabi's outward expression of aesthetic values is based on Zen's metaphysical and spiritual principles but translates these values into artistic and material qualities. Sabi suggests natural processes that lead to irregular, modest and ambiguous objects. The objects reflect the universal flow of "return" and "return". However, they indicate sufficient and provocative immutability, leading the viewer or listener to ponder and consider returning to the wab and again to wisdom, an aesthetic experience designed to create a holistic perspective that is calm and intuitive.

Objects in the Sab are irregular because they are asymmetric, modest because they are the whole fruits of the Wabizumi, obscure, preferring vision and intuition, evoking pure spiritual feelings rather than reason and logic. The ambiguity allows each viewer to continue their volatile abilities without excluding anyone or reducing the amount and quality of the experience.

Japanese poet Haiku Basho moved in wise poetry to an experienced wabizumai, and nature's melancholy became a kind of longing for nothing. But this longing, which was never fulfilled, "absolute" is not part of a woman's vocabulary: the tension between wab and sab makes for an enriching and incomplete experience.

Sabi is loneliness or even loneliness. It is an atmosphere created by poetry and music, a sense of art and drama, a reflection of landscapes. The principles of Sabie design have been applied to many Japanese cultural expressions, including gardens (zen and tea), poetry, pottery, calligraphy, tea ceremony, flower arrangements, bonsai, archery, music, and theatre.

The merger of Wab and Sab resulted in the use of two separate terms.
Wabi-Sabi

Here are two Juniper2 fragments that summarise the wabi-sab:

The term wabi-sabi refers to qualities such as persistence, humility, asymmetry and imperfection. These basic principles are at odds with Western colleagues whose values are rooted in a Hellenistic worldview that values stability, size, symmetry and perfection. ...

Wabi-Sabi is an intuitive assessment of the transient beauty of the physical world, which reflects the irreversible flow of life in the spiritual realm. It is a subtle beauty that appears in a humble, rustic, imperfect or even decadent aesthetic sensibility, and that finds melancholic beauty in the permanence of all things.

Contrary to Western aesthetic principles, its roots are in contrast to Western philosophical approaches to power, authority, control, commitment, and control, whether they be different or nature. The workmanship delivered by such a culture is a visual and contacting articulation of its qualities. The two cannot be separated. On the other hand, wabi and sabi usually do not differ in wabi-sabi art.

The principles of Wabi-Sabi design fall into several classes; Of course, visual arts such as poetry, drama and literature have no physical objects; expresses these principles in different ways:

type
form
structure
beauty
colour
ease
status
balance
moderation

TYPE

The materials used are organic, not synthetic. They can no longer be polished, cleaned or counterfeited to look new or redesigned. Therefore, wood, metal, paper, textiles, stone and clay contain acceptable materials that appear over time and that are clear and attractive to cross.

FORM

The subject has a natural or organic shape that indicates natural or intentional asymmetry or irregularity. The human impulse does not set the method, but it subtly intervenes to follow the talents and physical attributes of the character, the characteristics and the relevant preferences. This naturalness of shape is probably the first and most surprising feature of the object. First of all, work itself is not a symbol of anything.

TEXTURE

Depending on the material used, the surface remains rough, uneven, varied and random, and every aspect carries out a natural process.

BEAUTY

The aforementioned Western standard of grace cannot find a place in the wabi sab. Even traditional standards of beauty in people's minds, unknown in theory, are not necessarily Wabi-Sabi. Wabi-Sabi gives the visual and sensual permeability its absolute nature so that the fragility and vitality of the lost beauty over time is realised in today's state. The object reveals its different sense of beauty in subtle and even subtle details. Still, it is a holistic experience that is difficult to provide the abstract viewer with more information that conveys a particular sensitivity.

The wabi-sabi artist does not claim that the viewer "abstracts" something. Wabi-Sabi is a holistic experience, and objects decode the beauty of transferred feelings, not of any particular work. In this last sense, vision expresses itself more efficiently in a literary, theatre or ceremony experience than other principles.

colour

The subject does not care about anything loud or unnatural. Therefore, the colours are off. The light is diffused or dim. Colours are derived from natural sources, without any uniformity or unevenness. None of

the acoustic signals is conveyed solely by visual arts, such as the poem by Jakuren (12th century), quoted by Juniper:
Be alone
It's colour
cannot name:

This is the mountain where the cedars rise
It is dusk

EASY

Straightforwardness passes on the immediacy of characteristic materials that can't or cannot be decorated. The lack of contamination and the bottom confirm the authenticity of the work and its consistency with the spirit of Wabi-Sabi.

STATUS

Although the purpose of my work is to defend the wabi in the area, this area is about relationship and perspective. Nothing is wasted, but there is plenty of space around the object, which conveys a holistic philosophy in which all the elements are entwined and relevant to the whole. The landscape becomes the economy of the region (teahouse, bonsai), but space

conveys the nature of the universe (bowl or cup, archery, student garden).
stabilisation

The work reflects the physical balance of nature. Therefore, no predetermined symmetry formula is durable because of the quality of the conditions: wood grows tall or short, thin or thick, hardwood, distorted, etc. In connection with other trees, rocks, water, etc. soil, hummus, etc. in the forest. This balance of circumstances is the designer's principle for the artist's involvement in the work. Work like wood is unique. The regularity, uniformity and recipes created by the artist are secondary to the fact that it reflects the natural rather than forced appearance of the object and its context.
MODERATION

Tranquillity is a simple principle that art is sometimes defined better than what is left behind than what is introduced. Restraint adds a feeling of point of view to the experience of non-presence. The artist approaches the creative work with humility, honesty and clarity of motives. False motives poison art and inevitably be revealed at work. The artist must continue to create freely and intimately a personal and vulnerable work that is naturally full of Wabi-Sabi spirit. Sobriety offers ambiguity when the artist recognises her limitations and refrains from making bold or exaggerated statements.

Root finds it particularly useful to distinguish between the Wabi-Sabi principles and the principles of modernist art, as this minimalism is often confused with the Wabi-Sabi laws. Its theme comes from the horrendous experience of witnessing wabi-sabi, which is increasingly being rejected in Japan through the direct adoption of Western pop art and technology. The root table (edited here) takes advantage of the useful differences between modernist minimalism and wabi-sabi principles, which further clarifies the principles of wabi-sabi design.

But perhaps the best expression of the wabi-sabi aesthetic principles come from the practitioner, in this case, the bonsai practitioner, Peter Chan3, who distils several essential principles from many theoretical aspects.

Seven aesthetic principles

Chan's aesthetic principles are seven. The three basic principles are simplicity, tranquillity and naturalness.

Simplicity is a minimal and appropriate application. However, they no longer need the depth of aesthetic experience. Silence suggests the recovery and touch of a state that is comfortable and peaceful, without emotion or excessive stimulation. It is natural to avoid the invention. The artist tries to make the work look like it has always been a part of nature as if human interference had never happened. The plant (garden, path, even fence) seems to be a favourable result of natural disasters.

Two wabi principles are derived from wabi: no attachment and subtle depth.

The lack of attachment gives the work a fresh and original feel. The subject is somehow familiar, but it doesn't depend on anything else. Subtle depth is the concept of gravity. Chan calls it "a hint of emptiness." The term inexhaustibility is better than Wordsworth's "immortality" because here the object resonates within and within with endless possibilities and subtleties, hidden and revealed successively.

Of course, there are two basic principles: strict sublimity and asymmetry.

Asymmetry rejects the form of symmetry and balance to reconcile nature. It is the balance of an object in terms of space, place and relation. As stated, this is contrary to historically Western aesthetics, where painting, music and poetry fall into almost mathematical terms of symmetry. Fixed height reduces the object and its context to what is essential. All unnecessary elements burden the viewer and disturb the aesthetic experience, so an object that is now lacking in accessories carries the sublime. It's minimalism, but it's not modernism at all. Tight sublimity maintains a strong sense of emotion.
summary

Of course, aesthetic principles are still abstractions if they are not applied as much to our lives as to art. The application can be created when searching for different techniques or building elements in the everyday environment. While aesthetics can cause us to change relationships with material objects in our daily lives, they must provide an essential insight into our culture. The principle of simplicity, organic sources, and harmony with nature have practical applications to the philosophy of life and what may be called the philosophy of loneliness, the politics of simplicity, or even the politics of hermitian. As Juniper says,

The Wabi sab, as a tool for meditation and philosophy of life, can now play an unexpected role in counteracting the magnificent evolution of the social fabric that holds us for so long. Its principles of modesty and simplicity promote disciplined unity and prevent excessive descent into the physical world. It gently encourages a life of peaceful meditation and a soft aesthetic that emphasises a meditative approach. Wabi-Sabi demonstrates the role of intelligence and develops an intuitive sense of life where people and their environment must be in harmony. Embodying the soul to remind you of your mortality can increase the quality of human life in a universe that is quickly losing its otherworldliness.

The relevance of wabi-sabi in the past

Wabi-sabi gives approval after the effect of the program, and nothing

When a favourite cup of tea or a cup of beloved coffee falls and breaks, it is likely to be thrown away, a loss of feeling, waste and remorse. However, there is another way in Japan: to bring it back and proudly reveal the exact location where the fracture occurred. This policy sends a special message: imperfections can be a wellspring of pride. Barbara Bloom, an American craftsman, intrigued by Japan, summarizes it wonderfully: "The Japanese accept that when something is harmed and has a history, it becomes more comfortable."

Japanese kintsugi art, which respects incomplete, incomplete and aged people, is part of a broader philosophy called wabi-sabi. In free translation, "wabi" means simplicity and poverty, and "Sabi" may refer to the natural progression of time. Or, as Leonard Koren, an American artist, aesthetic expert, and author, calls it "the beauty of imperfect, unstable, and imperfect things" (Wabi-Sabi for Artists, Designers, Poets, and Philosopher, 1994).

In other words, wabi-sabi means deep acceptance of change and the certainty of death. The entirety of this is profoundly established in Buddhist way of thinking.

Love drawing mounted

"Forget your perfect offer. Everything has a crack. It comes to light," Leonard Cohen once wondered at the value of imperfection. However, it took ten years for the song to be completed, which questions: maybe he was a perfectionist himself?

Our modern world is projecting the unrealistic dream that things should be soft and stylish and not polished and rusty. Most of us strive for decent jobs, perfect body, perfect skin, ideal husbands and wives, and of course, smart offspring. If there is patience, we do not value or emphasise these moments. Instead, we seal them with a carefully packaged "Private" label.

The media often promote the notion that one can have everything: a decent and well-paid job, a warm house with organic and homemade meals, a head full of shiny hair and always a youthful complexion. Although change has dominated our whole lives, there seems to be no place to appreciate the time.

British master Alan Watts (often referred to as the forerunner of Western Buddhist teachings) remarkably skilfully remarked: "It is a contradiction if we want to be sure of a universe that is current and fluid. But the contradiction is a little deeper. , and I want to stand out from life. To understand music, you have to listen to it. But as long as you think, "I listen to this music, you don't listen" (Wisdom of Uncertainty: A Message to the Anxiety Period. 1951).

Nature follows

What's more, nature itself is the best educator of wabi-sab. For example, seasonal instability reminds us that everything on this planet is transient. Yes, there are flowering times: spring and decay, which occur in winter. The natural cycle can best be demonstrated through the symptoms of old age: rust, mould and mildew.

We, Westerners, are often ashamed to look at slightly damaged objects. However, the Japanese believe they have a connection with old and incomplete matters. Dried leaves, cracked pottery, fallen trees or uneven floors in an old house all the time evoke feelings of melancholy.

The great Japanese writer Tanizaki Jun'ichirō explained in 1933 the praise of the shadows for Japan's love of simple things: "We do not love all that is brilliant but prefer deliberate glow in the light, dim light that reveals ancient splendour. He adds," We love things where there are soot and the weather, and we love the colours and the brightness that remind us of the past that created them. "Basically, through the wabi-sabi lens that surrounds us, at home, in the city, or at work, we can be a source of beauty.

Local beauty notes

In 1859, Darwin discovered that people around the world define physical attraction according to local criteria. For centuries, beauty ideas blended with personality traits in Japan. The most interesting women were subtle and insidious in their physical and character traits. However, the Japanese bubble economy of the 1980s, combined with imitation of the world media, created a much more modern type of beauty. Suddenly, the perfect woman began to resemble the little Lolita of the anime: wide eyes, enormous bosoms and long legs.

At that point, during the 1990s, another promoting term, bihaku, meaning "beautiful white," took up the local beauty salon and sent many Japanese women into a twisting cream. Clear skin is distinguished by its purity, class and proximity to the type of Caucasian beauty. To date, bleaching products have dominated the Japanese leather industry and women's magazine advertising pages. This culturally built obsession with whiteness is so magnificent that there are even products for whitening nipples and intimate parts. They originate from the ancient Japanese popular belief that the skin of attractive women in these areas darkens. A few years later, the reaction to the idea of light skin was in the girls' subculture, called ganguro (translated: witches). They rebel against whitening by tanning their skin and dressing in African-inspired clothes. The cold died in the late 2000s.

White picture

Beauty is a complex concept; even more, than it has become a huge commodity. The West is obsessed with staying young through plastic surgery. This is a growing industry that is treating people as young as 25 on the verge of ageing. Interestingly, ageing in Japan is more subtle but less feminine. They grow up thinking that thin and white is the ultimate goal of beauty. Many of them blindly believe in the ageing power of the traditional diet based on soy and expensive cosmetics.

This hyper body variety in Asia cannot be compared to beauty-obsessed countries such as the United States or Australia. In fact, as American anthropologist and linguist Laura Miller points out in Beauty Up Exploring Contemporary Japanese Japanese Body Aesthetics, there is more Japanese work in the beauty industry than in combined wedding, funeral, car and IT services.

The Japanese do not seem to be familiar with the Western term "body image". Your language doesn't even have that word. In the United States and Europe, 'body image' refers to the physical appearance of self-perception and reaction to the demands of society. But in Japan, what others think is more important than understanding. People believe that the physical body, called karada, has no limits and is an empty fluid reservoir that is constantly changing.

Therefore, ageing gracefully looks more natural in Japan than in the West. The Wabi-Sabi approach to time means that a certain age opens women to new age-specific events. So, for example, as they grow older, they have more freedom to spend time and have fun. There is also a deep sense of community that unites women of the same age. They volunteer, buy and go to the sauna together. Social sauna, which in Japan is known as naked, accompanied, as the thermal waters, onsen, rarely allow the mixing of gender, is a place where the different life stages of women share their experiences.

I've often seen naked Japanese women in public toilets. They spent hours swimming, chatting and then brushing and combing French women's activist Simone de Beauvoir wrote in The Coming of Age: coexistence of fat and skinny, young and old, new and wrinkled.

Wabi-sabi me?

Imagine honouring the time you spent only with pottery, buildings or magazines that were too old in the fall, but only with the human body. French women's activist Simone de Beauvoir wrote in The Coming of Age: "Age is particularly difficult to assume because we have always considered it a foreign species, a foreign species." He published this statement in 1970 at the age of 62.

Maybe Japan's role in spreading the wabi-sabi concept of ageing? It is already one of the fastest ancient societies on earth. Individuals more than 65 record for a fourth of the population and will soon reach 40%. Modern scientific and technological inventions can delay the ageing process, but why don't we feel it? Or do you appreciate, like a cracked gold bowl, the enjoyable experience it was?

The relevance of wabi-sabi today

The West embraced wabi-sab in the form of personal development philosophy. However, it began as an approach to the concept of beauty by combining "wabi" (which can be translated as something approaching unfortunate intonations) with "Sabi" (referring to the effects of the passage of time).

Somehow wabi-sabi is a simple glimpse of reality; accepting that nothing stays the same and that change is at the heart of things.

The philosophy of anaesthesia has shifted from Zen Buddhism.

Wabi-Sabi dates back to Murat Jukō, a 16th-century Zen woman who transformed a luxurious tea ceremony into a peaceful and relaxing experience, focusing on purification through simplicity, using the essential handmade tools instead of the advanced dishes and deliberately demonstration services that were then.

The Wabi sab gradually became an art of living, and its influence extended to skills, interior design, style and thinking.

Another way to see the Japanese miracle

American craftsman Leonard Koren, who established WET Magazine, a gladly engaged hedonistic magazine focused on gourmet spa art, introduced wabi-sabi in the West in the 1980s. And back from San Francisco to Tokyo, he began producing anthropological works in view of the speciality of living, and in 1988 distributed 283 valuable thoughts from Japan, a sort of elective guide to economics and society designed for the United States, which he longed for success got rid of their organisational systems and performance criteria. He just believed that Japan could increase and strengthen its influence because of its deep-rooted cultural foundations, instead of gaining access to the industry because industrial models were at some point supposed to reach their limits.

The Metaphysics of Integrity.

So what are the solid cultural foundations that can cope with the significant changes in economic and social paradigms? The metaphysics of honesty is a summary of its roots: peacefulness filled with a form of spirituality; Whoever seeks simplicity, welcomes imperfection and sees change as an integral part of the life of being and doing.

In Wabi-sabi, failure is not bad, and old age does not mean aggravation and injuries do not mean harm:

we are beings, and we are alive, just inevitably marked and transformed by catastrophes, cracks, changes, etc.

Wabi-Sabi for personal development

As we look for ways to breathe and release, ways to increase our tolerance, accept ourselves and the world around us, recognise that we have the right to make mistakes and make the right changes in the workplace, I know that is very attractive. Its transition to personal development involves rejecting perfectionism and gaining humility. And it can be applied to our own lives (assuming there is no need for a flawlessly decorated showroom, and by dismissing the gruelling vision we always want to do better, we have already covered it in the Super Woman complex!) And our working life (assuming, may not be exceeded!).

Back to basics! Wabi-Sabi is to listen to and satisfy our exact needs and get rid of all irrelevant duties and responsibilities. And it starts with the way other people look at us, or rather the way we think they see us. And when we do, it's about putting an end to other people's guesses and expectations, leaving them room to express their needs openly.

Wabi-Sabi also encourages kindness. Self-esteem (the person who looks at you in the mirror is not that bad if you look at them with compassion) and serves others (they are who they are, with their unique characters, not just the features and weaknesses of the list).

It is about allowing yourself to enjoy the pure miracle. This does not mean over-enthusiasm, which can sometimes take too much energy and be invasive. It's just a joy to think about reality sentimentally, to take in the emotions that arise, to experience the dynamics that a gentle attitude can bring, sweet nostalgia for listening to children's songs, a sense of good news, or a sense of calm that provides an attractive frame.

What is / not is wabi sabi

To its purest essence, wabi-sabi is a Japanese art that finds beauty in the deficient and the depths of nature, comprising the natural cycle of growth, decay and death. It's dull, slow and neat, and everything gives authenticity. Wabi-Sabi is flea markets, not warehouses; old wood, not Pergo; Rice paper, not glass. Commend breaks and fissure and the various intimations left behind by the use of time, time, and love. It reminds us that on this planet, we are all just transient beings, that our bodies and the surrounding material world are restoring the dust we have come from. Through Wabi-Sab, we learn to absorb liver spots, rust and cracked edges and the progression of time they represent.

Wabi-Sabi is an underestimated and quiet, serene and dark beauty who is patiently waiting to be revealed. It's an incomplete vision: a branch that represents the whole tree, Shoji screens that filter the sun, the moon 90 per cent hidden behind cloud belts. It's richly soft, eye-catching beauty, but it's not clear that you can imagine being around you for a long, long time: Katherine Hepburn vs Marilyn Monroe. For the Japanese, the difference between Kirei, simply "beautiful" and omoshiro, is the one that throws something into the realm of beauty. (Omoshiroi means "white face", but its meaning varies from fascinating to fantastic). It is moss in the garden that quenches the smell of geranium, the astringent taste of green tea powder. My favourite Japanese phrase to describe wabi-sabi is "natsukashii Furusato", or the ancient memory of my hometown. (This is a typical pattern in Japan when people born in large urban areas, such as Tokyo and Osaka, become nostalgic for grandparents' rural homes that may never have been. Grandparents living in country prototype homes can even rent them.) And spend the weekend there.)

Daisetz T. Suzuki, one of Japan's leading English-language authorities on Zen Buddhism and one of the first scholars to interpret Japanese culture to Westerners, described wabi-sab as "an active aesthetic understanding of poverty." He did not mean poverty not in the form we understand (and fear) in the West, but in the most romantic sense, by removing the enormous weight of material concerns from our lives. "Wabin is content with a small cabin, a room with two or three mat mats like Thoreau's log cabin," he wrote, "and a plate of vegetables harvested from a field in the neighbouring countries, and maybe he hears a splash. Mild spring rains."

In Japan, a distinction is made between Wabibito (a Wabi person), who is similar to Thoreau in his heart, and non-Hindu Makoto, a more Dickensian character, because of the failed circumstances that make him desperate and unhappy. Read the ability to survive less; I've heard that someone mentions wabbit on as someone who can do something that is completely divided into eight parts when most of us would use ten. For use in the West, it may mean choosing a smaller house or smaller car, or merely a way to start refusing to add our potatoes.

The words wabi and sabi are not always linked, although they have been together for so long that many (including D. T. Suzuki) use them in the same way. The tea teacher with whom I spoke urged me to use the term wabi-sabi because he believed marriage would resolve their separate identities; The Kyoto master laughed and said she was together because it sounds like Ping-Pong. The two words have different meanings, although most people do not entirely agree on what they could be.

Wabi comes from the root wa, which refers to harmony, peace, quietness and parity. As a rule, wabi had the first importance of being miserable, deserted, and lonely, but poetically meant boring, immaterial, humble by choice and in harmony with nature. Someone who is ideally alone and who never wants something else is described as a wabi. Sixteenth-century teamer Jo-o described a person using wabi tea as someone who does not feel dissatisfied, even though he does not have Chinese facilities for drinking tea. The general phrase used in connection with Wab is "the joy of the little monk with his embroidered tunic". The Wabi person employs Zen, which means very little; free from greed, laziness, and anger; and understands the wisdom of rocks and grasshoppers.

Until the 15th century, when Japanese society admired the priests and hermits for their profound parsimony, wabi was a disparaging term used to portray happy and miserable renewers. Even today, the shades of desolation and rejection cling to words that are sometimes used to describe the feeling of helplessness you have while waiting for your lover. It also includes a touch of dissatisfaction with the unjustified criticism of lust and distraction, which was a vital sign of the ruling classes when the wabisuki (wabi flavour of all things) exploded in the 17th century. In a country dominated by warlords who were expected to appear to consumers, wabi is known as "aesthetic people," in the form of everyday samurai lifestyles that are undermined by material benefits.

Sabi itself means "flowering of time". Says that natural progression (spots, unevenness and rust) once turned off the brightness of the person who shone. It is the perception that beauty is transient. The meaning of the word has changed over time, from its old definition of being desolate to more neutral ageing. During the thirteenth century, Sab's purpose was to enjoy old and faded things. The proverb grew: "Time is friendly to things but cruel to people."

Sabi's dignity and grace take the most of the years: the oxidised silver cold, the interconnected surface, the grey colour rendering, the elegant drying of the fallen autumn. An old car that was left in the field to rust when it turns from eye to eye can be seen as the United States' contribution to the development of the exhibition. When an abandoned barn collapses, contains this mysticism.

The things that bear this patina are painful poetry, and it transcends Japanese. Americans are attracted to the relatively old European cities with their cobblestone streets and their cut mortar - places that are told much more rooted in the story than ours. We look for Sabia in antiques and even try to produce it in messy furniture. However, you cannot get real sab. It's a gift of the time.

So now we have a wabi that is modest and straightforward and Sabi that is rusty and worn. And we have published these expressions in a phrase that comes out of a language like Ping-Pong. So does this mean that the Wabi-Sabi house is full of simple, ordinary, rusty and tired things? That's the simple answer. In practice, however, the combination of Wab and Sab requires much deeper.

Debuting at home, wabi-sabi inspires minimalism that celebrates man, not a machine. Assets are reduced and returned to steam until only those that are necessary for their usefulness or beauty remain (preferably both). What do they cut? Things you love and use, such as hand eggs, that still work well. Items that are in harmony with the hands and heart of their creators: a chair made by your grandfather, the tubers of your six-year-old son, an Afghan who weaves himself (perhaps from worn sheep wool). Parts of your story: old photos with old sepia, baby shoes, Nancy Drew's puzzles that you read again and again as a kid.

The Wabi-Sabi décor is usually extinguished, dimly lit and shaded, and radiates rooms that give the uterus a sensation. Natural materials which are sensitive to weather, shrinkage, cracking and peeling give air pollution. The palette is drawn in brown, black, grey, earthy green and rust. This represents a lack of freedom but also an opportunity for innovation and creativity. There are hundreds of different shades of kimono in Japan. You have to respect your vision.

So you can see and feel them.
WABI, not SLOBBY

Wabi sab can be used in every way possible, and one of the most convincing is to use an excuse to exclude a defective bed, dirty floors or dirty couch. "Oh, that. Well, it's just wabi-sabi." My nine-year-old son Stacey loves this tactic.

How enticing it is let an area of a cushion on the sofa leave the seam to continue happily, calling it a wabi sab. Spend Saturday afternoons in theatres and let the dust settle on the carpets: wabi-sabi. Buy five minutes more sleep each morning without a bed by of course putting on wabi-sabi. Also, how would you know when you have gone too far as you have moved from pure, peaceful and rustic to anxious Uber?

The solid yellow line separates tortured and cloudy, dust and dirt from something worthy of worship. Wabi-Sabi is never messy or messy. Tired things get their magic only in situations where it is clear that they do not get into insects or dirt. It has been heard that they survived the times precisely because they have been treated so well for years. Even the rarest and more expensive antiques never play well in a house that is full or dirty.

Cleanliness means respect. Both ancient and modern tea masters have taught that even the neediest of wabi tea should always use fresh green bamboo and new white fabrics to wipe the teacup. In tea, the purity of the host is seen as a clear indication of his state of mind and commitment to tea. The tea book Chanoyu Ichieshu, published in 1956, goes so far as to advise guests to look for the host's toilet if they want to understand his mental training.

I do not support this extreme. I'm sick of the idea that anyone who evaluates me käymälöideni condition. But the point of the tea-master is worth it: carefully and beautifully cleaned spaces are ultimately more comfortable. When the bed is neatly made, it romanticises the collapsed blanket. The number of knots and cracks on the wood floor glows as the crumbs erupt. A clean but faded carpet that is tossed on the sofa and shows too many stains, makes it an irresistible resting place.

The roots of Wabi-Sab are in Zen Buddhism, brought from China to Japan by a 12th-century monk, Eisai. Zen, with its principles of enormous emptiness and nothing sacred, emphasises compassion, communication with nature, and above all, respect for everyday life as the real path to enlightenment. To gain understanding, female monks lived an ascetic, often isolated life, and sat for a long time in focused meditation.

To help their alien monks stay awake during these intense meditation sessions, Eisai taught them how to turn tea into hot drinks. When Eisai was gone, tea began a completely different life. Around the fourteenth century, the high societies created complex rituals that included tea. Famous tea houses are built in an enchanting style called rails, numerous Chinese hanging rolls and formal arrangements of flower vase tables and incense. Tea makers have demonstrated their wealth and position on three-day weekends with stylish Chinese-style tea accessories serving a hundred cups of tea - as well as food and sake.

Then came Murata Shuko, an influential tea master who is also a Zen monk. With the disappearance of the radical, Shuko began to use shabby, locally-made tools to socialise with tea. Saying "it is great to attach a commended pony to a straw house," he combined the coarse, ordinary products with familiar Chinese accessories, and the striking contrast made both look more interesting. Shuk's successor, Jo-o, was increasingly critical of men whose enthusiasm for rare or famous accessories was their primary motivation for drinking tea. Jo-o started with daily items such as a menu, a wooden bowl to feed pilgrims, a sewage tank, and a water tank of Shigaraki onioke, a silk dye bucket. He brought unpainted celadon and Korean peasant products into the classroom.

Still, Jo-o's disciple Sen no Rikki has allowed setting up a quiet, simple ceremony that allowed everyone, not just the wealthy, to use tea. During the sixteenth century - the beginning of a period of peace after many long civil wars in Japan - eating food was a rage, and Rikyu Tea became an oasis of calm, pure taste. He drank tea in bowls made by anonymous Korean potter and indigenous Japanese artisans, the most famous of which was the Raku family style. He made small cabins for tea (one and a half mat mats, unlike four and a half and up to eighteen carpets, which were the norm), based on a traditional village homemade of coarse mud walls, salt mats and organically shaped bare wood. The cabin had a nigirizushi, a low entrance that forced guests to bow and experience humility as they entered. Rikyu made some of his bamboo utensils (as common as a pond in Japan, but today, Rikyu is as original as Leonardo da Vinci's painting), and he arranged the flowers and of course the bamboo in the vases (shakuhachi) and basket. The Rikyu ceremony became known as wabichado (Chado means "tea") and has lasted to this day in Japan.

We, Westerners, tend to scratch their heads thinking of spending four hours on their knees, embarking on an elaborate ritual of making a charcoal fire, serving seasonal sacks, making one glass of green tea and distributing it to guests, and then making individual meals with a little sparkling water. However, most of us do not realise that tea embodies so much beauty that forms Japanese culture. To truly understand, you also need to study poetry, art, literature, architecture, heritage and history. The teapots deal with floral art, excellent food and - perhaps most importantly - a saree. And the four principles of composing the four teas (wa), reverence (kei), purity (sei), and serenity (active) can, of course, be an instrument for a good life.

Tea, in its current form, was born of a medieval society full of terrible war conflicts, but the samurai was willing to defer his deeds - and his swords - to become equal in the classroom. The design of the room is intentionally clean and bright; it was meant to be a sanctuary. "There should be no dust in that straw house; both the master and visitors are expected to be sincere. Normal proportions or etiquette or conventionalism do not have to be followed," says Nanboroka, one of the oldest and most essential tea books. "The fire will light, the water will boil, and the tea will be drunk; this is all that is needed here; other people's thoughts must not be disturbed." As soon as we enter the classroom, we are asked to let go of our problems and concerns and connect with others, "facing the harmonious, word-loving."

"Tea brings people together in a dangerous place to flee the modern world. Then they can come back and bring it with them," Gary Cadwallader, an American-born theme teacher teaching at the Urasenke Center in Kyoto, told me. I can't help thinking that we Americans who don't have the time - or do not want - to learn tea can take the heart of the statement and apply it to our own lives.

"If a friend visits you, make tea for him, welcome him warmly," wrote Jo-o, one of Japan's earliest tea makers. "Place flowers and make her comfortable." This is manifested in the typical Japanese phrase "Shaza Cat" which means "Well, sit down and drink tea". What if we accept this expression and learn to pronounce it more often - when our kids come home from school (before hurrying to hockey and ballet) when our neighbours stop when we are upset when the spouse starts growing up? If we were just allowed to stay for a moment, sit down together and have a cup of tea, what could that moment bring?

As we study tea, we are constantly reminded that every encounter is an endless opportunity to appreciate great organisation, excellent art, and some tea. We never comprehend what will happen tomorrow or even later today. Stopping Whether it's so important (meals, paying bills, working hours) exchanging conversation and a cup of tea with your loved one - or maybe your lover - is an easy way to advance harmony. It is from this spot of peace, agreement and friendship that the true Wabi-Sabi spirit is created.

Wabi-Sabi is not a decorative "style" but a way of thinking. There are no regulations; We cannot hang crystals or move beds and wait for the peace that will happen to us. The creation of a Wabi-Sabi home is a direct consequence of the wabi evolution, that is, the wabi development of the mind and heart: to live modestly, to learn to be content with life, as it can happen when we remove unnecessarily, to live instantly. Do you see it? Just as.

This is difficult in any culture, but in our environment, it is almost impossible. Every day in America, we come across sales points that help us improve ourselves, our conditions, our homes. We can have the smallest teeth, the cleanest carpets and the most significant off-road money we can buy. Everything flies in front of a wabigokoro, as described in Rikyu's text for the holy tea, Nanporoku. "A proud house and a taste of delicacies are just pleasures of the earthly world," he composed. "It is sufficient if the house doesn't spill and the food is hungry. This is the Buddha's teaching - the true meaning of Chad."

This is non-American. Or is it? I believe we all need something more profound than worse teeth, shining floors and eight chambers. Imagine a scenario where we could figure out how to be content with our lives. Just as they are today? It is an overwhelming idea, but one that is definitely worth the fun.

CHAPTER TWO

Culture

Every time I read the reviews on spiritual emptiness of consumption and well-known diagnoses massikulttuurista, which are more or less accurate, I am often depressed. After all, the superficiality of consumer culture is an everyday reality in our lives. It is always available, highly advanced and highly authoritative. On the contrary, no healthy and sustainable alternative has been defined. It seems that hiding "is not a series of negative aspects that call for cynicism, but it is not consistent and convincing" positive "that inspires its words.

It was interesting to learn about Leonard Koren's Wabi-Sab for artists, designers, poets and philosophers (Stone Bridge Press, 1994). The book is a brief poetic introduction to Japanese philosophy and aesthetics of wabi-sab. Wabi sab is not easy to summarise and is less articulate in rational language, but it presents a worldview that respects the humble and immediate, down to earth and incomplete. It is the sensitivity to live "here now" on a human level. It rejects the elegant and stable sensation of modern and market culture and celebrates the infinite beauty and grandeur found in small, ordinary, irregular and forgotten things.

The root holds a place in the design world, as does Christopher Alexander in design and Carlos Petrin in food and food. Everyone is a spiritual seer. Alexander is the author of A Pattern Language, a classic guide to elegant architecture, and Petrini is the originator of the Slow Food development, which emphasises the benefits of locally grown organic food and a friendly, long-lived diet. (Reporter Pilar Viladas has an excellent profile of Leonard Koren in the New York Times, October 9, 2005). I would like to know what these brave people could say during a wasted dinner (slow food, of course).

I wabi-sabi-neofyytti, so I request the correction, but Koren gives a convincing explanation of aesthetic hours, moods and attitudes. Wabi-Sabi is featured in family items, clothing, furniture, casual items, essential items and especially at a Japanese tea ceremony. Design principles celebrate minimalism but not asceticism. "Money is basically, but don't take away the poetry," Koren advises. "Keep things clean and messy, but don't sterilise them."

One of the goals of wabi-sab is to promote an understanding of the "evanescence of life" and the meaninglessness of traditional market groups and social life. Thus, Wabi-Sabi focuses on the "inner" and ignores the "material hierarchy," writes Koren. 'The normal hierarchy of material value about costs is not taken into account. Mud, paper and bamboo have the properties/values of wabi-sab made of gold, silver and diamonds. There is no "precious" in the Wabi sab because it would mean "not worth it". The subject receives the wabi-sabi status only when it is assessed as such. Wabi-Sabi content does not need to provide a market culture validation space. "

In addition to the aesthetics of design, wabi-sabi contains an implicit sense of the cosmos and the proper relationship between human beings and objects: "Wabi-Sabi is precisely the delicate balance between the enjoyment and the enjoyment of freedom." It is "a state of grace that has found a loud, humble and cordial intelligence. The main strategy of this survey is the media economy." E.F. Schumacher meets Gandhi?

Do ordinary goods have aesthetics? Why not, markets tend to promote a different view of space and people's satisfaction. Why is there usually no general orientation to life? Wabi-Sabi seems like an interesting version. It offers a sovereign view of "being in the world" and a sense of value in the market. Their sensibilities are morally reflexive, intuitive, and abundantly indicative of moderation, structure, and attraction. We could use more similar lighthouses.

What does "Japanese feel of flaw" truly mean?

Wabi-Sabi is a customary Japanese stylish idea that is regularly viewed as one of the most seasoned expressions of minimalism in art. But what is it? Indeed, even the Japanese are not entirely sure on the grounds that the express movement of Wabi-Sabi art has never happened, as has Impressionism or Pop art: people grouped specific arts afterwards and called them Wabi-Sabi, a term that consists of two ancient verbs. "侘 び (wabi) "and" 寂 び (Sabi.) "People today have only a vague idea of what means wabi and sabi because meanings have evolved over hundreds of years. Although wabi-sabi is still vague/challenging to understand the term, there are a few elements that will help you know or better understand what it is.

Wabi-Sabi was born sometime around the 14th and 15th centuries, during which Japan experienced drastic economic/social changes. First came an unprecedented accumulation of wealth. The devastating civil wars that caused regional army leaders to try to seize their wealth.

Zen heavily influenced the Wabi-saba, a new Buddhist school in Japan approved by military elites and soldiers.

S (Sado Tea Ceremony) is the most prominent Wabi-Sabi art that is a unique art of behaviour or attitude.

Wabi and Sabi mean: it is a Japanese version of "shocked" or "shabby chic".

As described above, wabi and sabi are two different ancient verbs that share standard features. Wabi (wabu) means to feel disappointed, upset or rejected. You can "wabu" if you force to live alone, away from home and family Sabu (Sabu) for degradation, degradation or oxidation. A single rock in a shaded area covered with old moss can be seen as "Sabu". If you love design or aesthetics, you may have already associated Western aesthetic quality with "problems" or "shabby style". Yes, like the shabby chic, wabi-sabi found beauty in expressions that were caused by wear or depreciation. But there's more to it than that. More than the physical appearance of old age, Wabi-Sabi contained both a source of beauty for philosophical imperfection and a sense of loss. And it is related to the social background that made the emergence of the Wabi-Sabi culture.

Zen and Wabi-Sabi

Understanding that everything created eventually disappears and that nothing is permanent and unconditional is, in fact, a central principle of Buddhism, called mu (Mujo). The strange thing about Buddhism is that the mujo was seen as a source of unlimited potential, not surrender. Everything in this universe travels every which way. Individuals, influence, cash, excellence are conceived, grow and die eventually. But death or fall also applies to the next birth/growth, and each of us who are part of this cycle of birth and degeneration plays a small but essential role in an infinite universe/universe that is continually growing in something of immense importance. Nothing has limitless potential even though I feel pain. Indeed, even before the Muromachi period, customary Japanese culture grasped and found beauty (the unconscious monkey) under challenging moments: people saw the many potentials as seasons, natural phenomena or relationships change, or as growth and maturity grow.

Then Zen took aesthetics from the most significant impression to the next level. Zen is a unique Buddhist school that focuses on meditation as an intellectual endeavour (there were tens of thousands of textbooks in Buddhism because of its very philosophical nature), which has a religious purpose, or Nirvana, which is the complete emptying of body and soul, pain or sorrow. Zen expanded its influence as new military leaders ruled overruling aristocrats after the 12th century and chose the physical and Stoic Zen for Buddhist school. The fact that Zen was based on stoic behaviours rather than intellectual efforts to find the truth had a significant impact on raising medieval philosophy and art to a high level of abstraction where the elements became essential. Words and meanings are removed, and objects are disassembled into pure components. Wabi-Sabi was born to discover the truth of this world. After all, all kinds of good and evil came and went.

Japanese Character

As indicated by Leonard Koren, wabi-sabi can be portrayed as "the most striking and characteristic feature of traditional Japanese beauty, and has roughly the same position in the pantheon of Japanese aesthetic values as the Greek ideals of beauty and perfection in the West." Although Andrew Juniper points out, "If an object or expression can arouse in us a sense of peaceful melancholy and spiritual longing, it can be said to be a wabi-sabi object." To Richard Powell, "Wabi-Sabi cherishes everything by recognising three simple realities: nothing lasts, nothing is complete, and nothing is perfect."

Wabi and Sabi are not easily translated. Wabi initially alluded to the forlornness of living in nature, far from society; Sabi means "cold", "thin" or "drained". Around the fourteenth century, these meanings began to change and became more positive connotations. Wabi now stands for rustic simplicity, freshness or tranquillity, and can be used in natural and artificial objects or subtle elegance. It can also refer to the peculiarities and abnormalities of the building process that add uniqueness and style to the purpose. Sabi is beauty or serenity that comes over the years as the meaning and permanence of life are manifested in its patina and wear or any visible repair.

After conquering artistic and Buddhist influences from China for centuries, the wabi-sab eventually became an unmistakably Japanese perfect. After some time, the implications of wabi and sabi have become cheerful and hopeful. About 700 years ago, especially among Japanese nobility, the understanding of emptiness and imperfection was valued as the first step toward a tent or enlightenment. In today's Japan, the meaning of wabi-sab is often condensed to "the wisdom of natural simplicity." Artbooks generally define it as "imperfect beauty".

From a design or design point of view, wabi can be interpreted as an imperfect quality of any product due to inevitable design and construction/manufacturing limitations, especially given the unpredictable or changing operating conditions. Sabi could be interpreted from the imperfect reliability or limited mortality of any object, resulting in a phonological and etymological connection with the oxidizable Japanese word Sabi (錆, also pronounced Sabi). Although kanji signs for "rust" are not identical in Sabi (寂) wabi-sab, the original spoken word (pre-kanji, Yamato-Kotoba) is thought to be the same.

Modern wabi-sabi kettle

A great example of this embodiment can be seen in the distinctive forms of Japanese ceramics. Ceramic items used in the Japanese tea ceremony were often rustic and dull in appearance, such as Hague articles, whose shapes are not entirely symmetrical, and colours or textures that appear to emphasise a pure or unclean style. Based on the knowledge and observations of the participant, hidden signs of truly magnificent design or enamel (similar to the appearance of a rough diamond) can be detected and detected. This can be interpreted as a kind of Wabi-Sabi aesthetic, which further reinforces the knowledge that enamelled articles change colour over time as water is repeatedly poured into them (Sabi) and the fact that teapots are often intentionally broken or cut. (wabi), which acts as a signature of the Hagi-Yaki style.

Wabi and Sabi suggest feelings of desert and loneliness. In the Mahayana Buddhist perspective on the universe, this can be considered as a positive attribute that represents the liberation and transcendence of the material world towards a simpler life. However, the Mahayana philosophy warns that genuine understanding cannot be achieved through words or language, so adopting wabi-sab in the non-verbal sense may be the most appropriate approach. Simon Brown [9] points out that wabi-sabi describes how students can learn to live life through the senses and participate more in life as it happens rather than grabbing unnecessary thoughts. In this sense, Wabi-Sabi is a material account of Zen Buddhism. The idea is that the environment of natural, changeable and unique objects will help us communicate with the real world and escape from potentially stressful distractions.

Silent Japanese words

Kandzis are the high condensers of meaning, symbols of complex emotions (sometimes even painfully explained) enclosed within a single sign (or pair).

For example, this linguistic particularity I have taken 9 Japanese expressions that can not be translated into a single word, and who speak the whole world in several kangeissa.

The monkey doesn't know

The monkey is not aware

It does not sound perfect. Still, it is one of the Japanese words which I love the most and represents the basic concept of the classical aesthetic of Japanese culture, which dates back to the Heian period (I have already written about this in this mailing Sakura as loss of consciousness monkey symbol).

The monkey but the conscious shows some nostalgia and sensitivity to the transition of beauty and life.

- Tsundoku

Ok, this is my word! When I write at a bookstore, I can't go without a book, even if I have other things to read, so I stack a lot of countless books!

- Satsukibare

The term "bright day in May" originally meant a sunny day in the rainy season.

It is presently used to allude to a day with a mainly clear sky in early May.

- Kawaakari

Seductively simple, with only the river and light canyons, this word, which is not translated, is one of the most attractive images in history. Just say it so you can imagine the whole scene and you want to be in front of a river lit by the sunset.

- Fuubutsushi

The three dog teeth, the wind, things, and poetry depict the nostalgia you know in the air that you can hardly express unless it is in Japanese.

- Komorebi

One of my favourite words: poetry locked in four characters.

- Wabi-Sabi

Non-transferable, wabi-sabi is a Japanese aesthetic concept, similar to the mono-conscious but more related to art, and refers to the beauty of imperfect things.

- Yuugi

The aesthetic principle associated with Wabi-sab is not only an immutable word, but it is also difficult to explain that the definition changes according to the context.

Yuugen means unimaginable depth and hidden beauty, the charm of dim things, which you cannot fully comprehend.

- Kintsukuroi

This means "repair with gold" and is part of the wabi-sabi aesthetic concept practice whereby the damaged object is not thrown but, on the contrary, treated and decorated by pouring liquid resin with gold dust cracks

Beauty does not live in perfection but in the history of life change and subsequent imperfection.

Objects, especially ancient pottery, have a temporal dimension, and each of them in a golden design of cracks tells a different and unique story, becoming a symbol of beauty.

CHAPTER THREE

Living with Nature

First, I studied the Japanese terms kintsugi (金繕い) and wabi-sabi (侘寂) from Candace Kumai, an internationally renowned chef and author of Kintsugi Wellness. Properly selected as the "golden girl of the well-being", Candace takes us on an inspiring journey as she explores her Japanese heritage in the hope of a personal loss of healthy mind, body and soul. In her book, she shares an assortment of cultural traditions and practices on healthy living as well as some of her favourite recipes using pure and natural ingredients.

What exactly are kintsugi and wabi-sabi?

Kintsugi is a stunning Japanese art form for repairing broken pottery. This is achieved by combining the pieces with varnish and filling the cracks with gold dust. Instead of trying to hide the shortcomings, Kintsugi encourages us to honour them. Uniting gold is something symbolic of its real value. It is a representation of something greater that was born of decay. We can incorporate this same principle into our daily lives through the Zen philosophy of "wabi-sabi", which teaches us to celebrate flaws. In the translation, wabi means "rustic simplicity" which "enjoys imperfection".

Take into account your shortcoming.

Go out, and you will find that nature is an excellent example of imperfect perfection. Trees can be twisted at odd angles with bent branches and have no symmetry marks, but are still considered beautiful. Even with ageing limbs and lost leaves, they leave a lasting impression on those who can appreciate them. Perfections are most valued because it makes them special and unique. The same concept applies to deficiencies.

Hold the Resistor.

If you feel any breakup, seek a peaceful centre and grow patience to withstand the challenging event. Try resisting meditation or breathing exercises to shift your focus. Remember that every golden crack is a symbol of courage and represents the beloved scars of a challenge that has been overcome. Be proud to show your flaws by sharing stories behind them and how you have recovered from your struggles.

Become a better version of yourself.

The renewed vitality and beauty come from the Kintsugi healing process. What used to be broken is becoming more and more critical and is considered to be more valuable because of gold mining. The problematic challenges he suffered and the deepest wounds he suffered are among the most beautiful. As you slowly rebuild your life, you can overcome the pain of creating a new life story and become a source of inspiration for others.

Practice self-esteem and forgiveness.

Today's society has high expectations of perfection through influence in all types of media. Although, indeed, no one is perfect or reaches his full potential because there is always room in life to reach higher limits. So be kind to yourself and accept who you are. Stop comparing yourself to others and practice self-acceptance. The unique qualities that make you less perfect define you.

Another essential concept in life is to forgive and give them certain things. Analysing useless little things can take a lot of time and energy. Do not quit in the past, but switch to the present and move toward a more positive light.

Using Kintsug and wabi-sab in everyday life can help us recognise our true beauty. Wabi-Sabi reminds us whether broken or broken, and our faults are a valuable decoration. Our cracks tell a more in-depth story on our journey and remind us that life is a process of continuous improvement. The confidence that the repair would heal us back to a stronger state, and the new gold stamps turned out to be a great reminder of our lives well.

Japanese aesthetic philosophy offers a new perspective on the so-called about our physical errors.

The Greek classic ideal of beauty, which favours much of Western physical aesthetics, spends steady and symmetrical perfection. Wabi-Sabi rewards authenticity; Cracks in an old cup look more like property than mistakes.

"Wabi-Sabi has a different look, a different way of thinking," says Robyn Griggs Lawrence, in a reprint of Simply Imperfect: Wabi-Sabi House. "It's about embracing the beauty of things as it is."

Still, wabi-sabi is more than a way of seeing things. It is "a lifestyle that values and embraces complexity while appreciating simplicity," writes Richard Powell in Wabi Sabi Simple. He says he accepts three simple realities: "Nothing lasts, nothing is complete, and nothing is perfect."

But because of this traditional Greek worldview, most Americans are distracted by things, even their bodies, that do not fit a particular ideal. This acceptance of the wabi-sabi look can be open to the eyes and mind.

By observing ourselves through this abundant lens, we can continually fight for an ideal body and focus on true physical health. All we need is an adjustment in observation.

Exceeding perfection

We all have things we dislike, aspects that we may not need to change. It can be a physical feature like big feet (hey, it would be me) or a way to go straight to the gym to go out with friends at night to enjoy a great daisy (hey, again). But obvious shortcomings are often our best parts, especially when viewed from a new perspective.

Even though it's not ideal, I know I should be a margarita after the gym than if I drank without it. And while big feet often made me feel safe in a gym where giant shoes stand out from my thin calves, they take me to New York almost every day, and it rarely hurts, even after one night of dancing with a 4-inch heel. Although I do not reflect my feet, I appreciate them.

Courageous souls sometimes turn their "imperfections" into signatures. "Ask yourself, 'What can I do miraculously in what I now call the wrong step? ", Wabi Sabi Love writer Arielle Ford suggests." And can you accept it? "Actor Lauren Hutton's lips and interdental space would become her business card." Many people would remove that mole and close it. Gap. Instead, they turned these defects into the property. "

Taking a Wabi-Sabi perspective does not mean lowering standards, but allowing you to see and treat your present self as it is.

Enjoy the process

"It's a process that happens in nature and then fails or dies," says Tony Burris, an acupuncturist in Boise, Idaho, who incorporates wabi-sabi concepts into his practice. "And we are not excluded from the process. The process is actually" there. "

For me, respecting the process meant accepting my attitude towards yoga neck support. I've practised for years, but because of an old neck injury that caused hermokivua arms and hands, I try to reproduce. It feels very risky. Although I have legitimate reasons to avoid it, I was afraid of the class support and found ways to fake it. Let's say baby posture or pretend to jump because I didn't want to accept what my body said.

Do I look at my yoga practice through Wabi-Sabi lenses and especially his view that everything is incomplete? In the process, I ended up not disturbing that I did not control this misleading pose. Presently I can unwind and appreciate the meeting.

"When you can accept things as they are, there is no judgment," says Lawrence. "You don't say, 'I should do less, weigh more, I wouldn't have these wrinkles,' but 'This is happening. "Suffering comes when one wants to be different. "

Accept the change

"Young beautiful people are natural disasters," said Eleanor Roosevelt, "but they are beautiful old works of art."

I remember this well because I notice that in addition to the wrinkles around my eyes, ageing is also visible in my hands. Thinner skin, which makes veins and bones more apparent, revealing small cracks on the skin surface. But I love hands. With the help of the keyboard, they give me a living. So I am grateful to them and treat them, spread the cream, rub them and give them breaks. I can hug them quickly.

In other words, I'm not even ready to imagine my hair dyed. However, many women fearlessly accept their silver thread. "The day I cut my coloured hair, the man stopped me in the street and asked me to bring Martin with me.

How to live in a wabi-sabi style and embrace imperfection

We live in a digital world where we almost wondrously see how other people live their lives, albeit through choices, and this can often be easily traced to personal inadequacy. Look! Your home is spotless! Your clothes are in fashion! Your kids are perfect! And we begin to fight for the hard level of error that we think others have.

However, what we frequently overlook is that no one is perfect, and these "on-screen" lives are rarely an accurate representation of reality, or at least the customised, not-so-glamorous elements of everyday life.

How to accept your lack

Instead, we must remember that it is our physical, mental, household and professional deficiencies and deficiencies that make people exciting, genuine and inspiring.

It recognises the beauty of deficiency that goes beyond the need for a perfect, perfect life and home, and we need to look at the Japanese wabi-sabi philosophy so we can start to take a different perspective and make changes to improve our self-esteem. And enjoy every day.

So what is the wabi-sabi lifestyle?

Wabi-Sabi Welcome writer Julie Pointer Adams describes it as "a lifestyle that celebrates complete imperfections: beauty found in unusual and contemporary places or objects that are sometimes overlooked or undervalued".

Aesthetically, it is a counterpoint to modernism: these are wrinkled cloth napkins, it is a very used and beloved leather bag, irregular surfaces, painted with ceramics. But it's not just a visual concept: we embrace a set of principles that can change the way we think about our lives.

It accepts us as it is, opening our homes to others without fear of being judged, appreciating what we have, without having to replace and update it regularly, and recognising the passage of time, its temporality, and its inevitable degradation.

Find the tribe on social media

Today, it is almost impossible to watch other people's lives through social networks. Still, instead of ultimately refusing to use platforms, it can be used as a way to drive change in your life by merely connecting with the right people.

Many bloggers and creators embrace wabi-sab and a slower lifestyle by openly sharing their experiences of living, decorating, and cooking. Often, honesty and openness can provide a source of inspiration and a sense of community.

Photographer, author, and mother of three, Emma Rice, says she's embracing the Wabi-Sabi lifestyle and hoping to inspire others to recognise the beauty of imperfection. "It's the way I've always lived, but later in life, I discovered why this word the way I saw the world in the past." I think wabi-sabi is a loving acceptance of imperfection.

"Because I am an imperfect human, like everyone else, and as a teenager kamppailisin dyslexia, ADD to and from specific mental health problems, it gave me all of a sudden way to look at myself and realise that all of these deficiencies were the only part of me and I could I would be myself as I am . "

Get inspired by nature

Emma did not personally apply the principles of wabi-sab, but also cooking, nurturing, decorating and training. In-home furnishings, he explains that nature has a strong influence: "Nature rarely draws a direct current. Even as complex as a spider web that has been inspected, it has natural flaws and is not completely geometric."

As Emma decorates, she is drawn to asymmetry, imperfect lines, robust texture, and natural colour palette. He also admits: "Cleaning leaves a lot to be desired! If I had a perfect and modernist house and everything was on track, it would shake, but when you don't want perfection, and you need it to be harmonious, it would be easier to maintain."

Emma's house is full of used furniture, mixed with natural textiles and handmade items she has collected over the years. At the centre of her kitchen is a large wooden table (flea track, torn and broken over time), the perfect place to meet your family for lunch.

How to Follow the Wabi-Sabi Lifestyle

Although Emma does not know any Japanese ancestor (though she wanted to!), Her father and grandparents lived for years in the early 20th century.

He grew up with the beautiful, lacquered tea caskets, pencils and ink drawings that his family had collected around his greenhouses.

He admits that his education probably had something to do with being part of Japanese culture, but explains that his current eating is that his own family was born out of necessity.

"I don't eat a lot of wheat, and when I found out that my son had a wheat tolerance, we started making family meals without grain.

"We also have a mix of vegetarians and fishermen in the house, so the concept of serving a big rice bowl surrounded by numerous small plates full of vegetables, grilled fish or meat, tofu or eggs meant that everyone could bring them the best food items." it happens that the Japanese serve and eat food. "

How wabi-sabi can improve your well-being

Emma also revealed that all prosperity developed in the practice of Tai Chin and Chi Gung (also known as 'Qi Gong').

He explains, "Chi Gung is a bit like meditation, but it emphasises slow movements that balance the energy of your whole body. I admire it, and it has helped me hugely in attempting to move on a somewhat destructive spiritual path. I think everyone should learn something, and we must have a peaceful spiritual place to return to today's busy world. "

As a working mother, Emma is easily subjected to the pressures of modern life. She does not tell the fact that she has often struggled with her mental health, but says that following the Wabi-Sabi principle allows her to balance her life.

His approach to social networks also changed: "The answer changed me when I was most honest on my Instagram feed. Don't misunderstand me, I love posting beautiful photos, but I started leaning on the raw and honest story with these photos.

"It seems to resonate and move people because I have had such a great answer. Some people may be wary of denying their souls online, but if they see others respect them and whose lives look good and are sincere, it permits People to love themselves and their shortcomings.

"This reflects the whole Wabi-Sabi principle that you still love yourself, even if you are not perfect."

Five principles live in a wabi-sabi style

Get rid of it

Reduce your living space, and this will help cleanse your mind.

Exit

Give yourself time to sit and think outside, among nature.

Live seasonally

See how the seasons come and go.

Take on the imperfect

Feel and love your flaws and try to love them in others.

Enjoy your feelings

Let yourself be melancholy or sad, enjoy it, we don't have to be happy all the time.

The beauty of imperfection

Wabi-Sabi is in fashion. This oriental philosophy now inspires a new design trend based on simplicity and natural materials and covers the flaws that surround us. But it is much more.

Wabi-Sabi cherishes everything genuine by recognising three simple realities: nothing lasts, nothing is complete, and nothing is perfect. "This is how Wabi-Sabi Simple writer Richard Powell summarises the essence of this philosophy in a way that is easy for our Western minds to understand. Since the term Wabi-Sabi is not translatable, it is difficult to explain, even to the Japanese.

What is Wabi-Sabi?

Its name comes from the translation of two complicated terms: "Wabi" (simplicity) and "Sabi" (age-related beauty or serenity). Together they are related to the beauty of imperfection. The starting point for this trend is Zen philosophy. It involves reaching a peaceful agreement, accepting unexpected events and life shortcomings, and enjoying the happiness of dull moments.

For artists, designers, poets and philosopher Wabi-Sab writer Leonard Koren, it is "the beauty of imperfect, unstable and imperfect things". This beauty of unusual things is accompanied by asymmetry, rudeness, simplicity and humility.

We can see the influence of Wabi Sab in several Japanese art practices, such as ikebana, haiku, pottery, gardening or tea ceremony. But especially in tin candies, the art of repositioning goods on valuable materials. The emphasis on imperfection rather than concealment adds to the beauty of the original and gives it new life.

We can see the influence of Wabi-Sab in many Japanese art practices such as ikebana, haiku, pottery, gardening and tea ceremony. But above everything is seen in kintsugi, the art of attaching objects to valuable materials. Flaws stand out instead of hiding, which adds to the beauty of the original item and gives it a new life.

Wabi-Sabi makes us happier

Wabi-Sab can be used in all aspects of life. If you pay attention, there are plenty of examples around you. Doesn't the recent trend of top model brands jeopardise models that are not such a perfect example of Wabi-Sab? Rebecca Marine's bionic hand, Winnie Harlow's vitiligo and Ashley Graham's weight are part of her beauty and the keys to her runaway success.

In addition to physical imperfection, it can also be the key to a happier existence. To accomplish flawlessness in our lives is a deception, and Wabi Sabi instructs us that there are things that we cannot change. The idea of imperfection is not only part of life, but it is also at its core, but it also helps us to resist failures and allows us to make mistakes. This is what psychologist

Tomás Navarro defends in his book "Wabi-Sabi, Learn to Accept Imperfection", saying that applying Wabi-Sabi's philosophy to our lives offers "a calmer approach that allows us to accept life as it is, not as we want it to be." The motto of Wabi-Sabi life would be "live in an instant. Carpe Diem!

Wabi-Sabi is the interior: nature and simplicity

It can be combined with slow design, Scandinavian hygiene concept, minimalism and mindset. But in reality, Wabi-Sabi is more complicated than all these because it comes from the philosophy of life. The key to incorporating it into your environment is to appreciate the simplicity and inspiration of nature, to reject unnecessary and artificial and to worship imperfection.

There are already several interior designers who have made Wabi Sabi the main principle of their work. Dutch designer Axel Vervoordt is one of them. In his book, Wabi Inspirations shows the sources of inspiration and the interior design of this philosophy. One of them is the Greenwich Hotel, located in the elite Tribeca district of New York. Working with Japanese architect Tatsu Miki, he wants to create a relaxing paradise for the city.

Wabi-Sabi inside in six stages.

There are numerous approaches to decipher this pattern, however, these are the six fundamental focuses for making a Wabi-Sabi interior.

Made from natural materials:

Wabi Sabi is inspired by nature and is based on the use of raw materials: wood, fabric, stone, ceramics, etc. They retain their imperfection and rustic quality, so they are used almost without treatment.

Use imperfect and direct objects or objects that have been exposed to weather conditions:

This is not about dressing artificially outdated fashion items, but about stripping your belongings or restoring your family property. Asymmetry and its finishing errors are also welcome.

Remove excess:

Forget visual and cumulative emphasis. It's not about "less is more". We should only have what is necessary, not more than less.

Natural Colors:

Natural shades appear, again and again, those that are consistent with the materials used and remind us of nature, such as earth, grey and white, without any savings.

Texture:

Wabi Sabi restores a sense of touch through surfaces already existing on natural materials: branches in wood, grains in stones, fabric in textiles. The good news is that wrinkles are also welcome as part of the imperfection. See you later, iron!

Decorative details:

For what? They fall into an unnecessary category. But if they are, they must be about nature: branches in clay boxes, shells, plants, etc.

The result is a simple, artistic, but also a warm environment that gives natural materials, textures and objects a personality.

Do you have enough games to try Wabi-Sab?

Wabi-Sabi is not just about accepting imperfection

"Perfection is not only a tolerable thing; it is a natural part of life that we must learn not only to recognises but even to celebrate! This view of wabi-sab encourages us to treat faults as a beautiful part of the whole.

For example, when a piece of pottery breaks in Japan, there is a beautiful process called kintsugi, which means "gold repair," where the crack solidifies with a gold-coloured stick. Rather than attempting to conceal the defect, the fix becomes more evident with the gold sticks passing through the ceramic. Likewise, wabi-sabi teaches us to re-examine what we generally consider to be the imperfection we want to dress and accept it as what makes the object, experience, or itself original. Things like an old dining table with wine-coloured wood, laughter lines around the mouth, or a hand-knit sweater with irregular dots. "

How does wabi-sabi fit into regular culture in these different places?

"Of course, I can talk more about how I experienced wabi-sabi in California, but I understand wabi-sabi is a concept so ingrained in Japanese culture that everyone knows what it is, but it's hard for them to describe it to the Japanese. : It is attention to detail, ephemeral, ceremony and most importantly, live and in harmony with nature.

The habit of witnessing the Wabi-Sabi state in Japan was mostly to see how people's homes were designed and inhabited. The houses where I spent my time were simple, sober, maintained by nature and modern in design, but also full of warmth and character. Although the objects and decorations were rare, the house was very personal, mostly handmade, inspired by nature, eclectic and carefully chosen. Each dish was a unique original, handmade, and although no dish or dish matched each other, the overall appearance was necessarily very uniform.

When it comes to California, the way people live in Wabi-Sabi is slightly different, as you might suspect. If the Japanese are known for their formality and precision: Imagine that the Japanese bow carefully and respectfully at their meeting; the Californians are the opposite. At least in California, I know that wabi-sab's shape is more comfortable to live in relaxed "hanging" with sand and floating wood passing through the house, randomly arranged as a sculpture. People find beauty in every day and moving moments of life, just like the Japanese. Nevertheless, it can be by following a surfer on the wave or grilling in the yard instead of performing a ritual tea ceremony or practising Zen Buddhism. "

What are the best tips to incorporate wabi-sabi into our day by day lives?

"Wabi-Sabi welcomes us to embrace current circumstances. It is a laid back, relaxed and realistic approach to life, but it is also not easy, it requires careful and loving attention to the world around you. An excellent place to start is to slow down and bite and start paying attention to the imperfect beauty all day long.

Another tip is to replace beauty with utility whenever you can, for example, look for a friendly storage basket, a beautiful water table can, or even a delicate toilet brush; Small things that change the way we live.

And finally, by doing what you adopt with wabi-sab, you recognise the beauty of ordinary and incomplete things instead of needing or wanting more. In this spirit, personalise your home with just the things you care about, such as family photos, travel memories, or art created by children. "

Wabi-sabi's character is human

The wabi-sabi (despicable beauty) nature of human behaviour has brought us the best stories in the world. The vulnerability unites us. The perfect hero is made for boring stories. We stand for the struggling hero and the profound insights that turn everything around.

The idea that we are Wabi-Sabi people has come to me in a profound moment of truth.

One day I would struggle with how to handle a particular situation. The opportunity to have a phone call with a colleague and found myself thinking, "I bet he always says the right thing at the right time. There seems to be a way with people. "

Such moments as my inner critic escaped like a destructive gin from a bottle can be the beginning of a tirade of how completely imperfect I am. It's rude. Tyrant offers examples of people who excel when he says, "You don't measure."

- But at this point, it was something different.

- The word dropped in my head.
- Wabi-Sabi. It continued. Wabi-Sabi. Wabi-Sabi.

My mind jumped on a food photography course where we stacked colourful macros on an old chopping pan. The comparison was perfect. The uneven patina of the soaked plate knocked on a craftsman t-shirt.

What have the empty trays to do with interrupting my inner critic?

Wabi-Sabi is a Japanese expression for discovering excellence in the imperfection of things, which is compiled into a mistake of beauty.

At the heart of the Wabi-Sabi concept is that nothing is ever perfect, nothing is ever complete, and nothing is permanent.
- Next came to my mind;
- To be human means to be wabi-sabi.
- Our nature as human beings is this;

We're not perfect. We shouldn't either. We are here to experience life so that we do not supplement the art of living.

We are never ready. Nor should we seek complementarity. The potential for development is endless and vast.

We're transient. We are in a constant flow state. At one point, we think and feel one thing, and the next moment, something else. This is because the idea passes through us. There is always a fresh set of plans.

But we hide from the world of our wabi-sabi world. We think our imperfect exterior is wrong and we need to fix it and make it representative. Instead of showing our unique patina, let's see how we can rise again.

We expect res looks like we just left the factory with a QC sticker that says good to go.

Everyday social media gives us a new way to stand out. Our feeds are full of articles listing 7, 12, or 101 ideas to become better people. They get millions of views and likes.

But here's the thing

The nature of the Wabi-Sabi human being is part of us that is imperfect, imperfect and ever-changing, and it builds our unique patina as we live our lives.

All our stories are from our wabi-sabi nature, and like that old baking tray orbits of wool or rusty old gasoline, you will find incredible beauty in them. When we tell our stories, we show our unique patina to others, and this opens the way for others to reveal their wabi-sabi character to us.

Wabi-Sabi's character turns against us when he takes it too seriously and begins to think that we are no longer the mole or scar of grazed knees or pines.

We have days when we seem to compare things and days when we miss a sign. Everybody does. Wabi-Sabi. It's life. We live and learn.

But we are more than people with wabi-sabi. There is also a part of us that is whole, perfect and continuous, and that is our spirit. Although our human nature is temporary, spiritual nature is eternal.

We are not people with spiritual experience; we are spiritual beings with human experience. Pierre Teilhard de Chardin.

So we are Wabi-Sabi people who are completely wrong and still perfect.

As people, our lives are comprised of stories, while spiritual nature is the space between our stories. As we share our stories, we connect resonance to the account and deeper into space from which the story emerges through the energy connection.

Everyone knows what a connection looks like, but it's hard to describe it as a chocolate flavour. In Tao of storytelling, I called that energy connection Tao.
We are not here to choose between our stories and space from which these stories originate. Music is

created through a note and space. We are a combination of our stories and the space between our stories.

So, paradoxically, we are Wabi-Sabi people with a wealth of stories, and yet we are perfect spiritual beings who are not affected by anything that has ever happened to us in our lives. The journey of our lives is not to choose between these fantastic aspects, but to dance between the two and respect each other with equal praise.

Moral precept of wabisabi

Wabi-Sabi is a natural way of life, its beauty that moves towards or from scratch. It is the beauty of imperfect, permanent, imperfect, humble, humble and unusual. The word wabi refers to a spiritual, subjective, philosophical and territorial path. Sabi refers to material objects, goals, aesthetic and temporal ideals.

Wabi-Sabi is very difficult to determine because nature is incomprehensible. This can only be found in your mind, and its sense of beauty cannot be described to anyone else. To know wabi-sab, you must see it, observe it, experience it and understand it yourself.

Wabi-Sabi has a rustic, primitive, down to earth, multicoloured, crude, natural, imperfect and even ugly beauty. This sets it apart from modernism, which is soft, minimalist, mechanical, perfect, polished, smooth and beautiful beauty. Although wabi-sabi is private, innovation is public. While wabi-sabi is intuitive, change makes sense: relative to absolute, personal to universal, unique to mass production. Wabi-Sabi is focused on the present, future-oriented innovation. The organic version is geometric, warm-cold, decomposition compared to maintenance, mostly dark compared to generally bright, seasonal or eternal. Wabi-Sabi is nature; Modernism is technology.

Wabi-Sabi is similar to modernism in the sense that both are abstract ideals of beauty. Both refer to objects, space and design. They are reactions to the dominant and established emotions of their time. They have nothing to do with decoration that is not part of the structure. They are recognised on the surface but have a deeper connection to the indescribable beauty.

Wabi-Sabi's metaphysical foundation is that things evolve from evolution to emptiness, that the universe is continually moving toward or beyond potential. These are sensitive traces of events or items that have become nothing or have not yet come out of nowhere. Nothing is space and something alive with opportunities.

The spiritual value of Wabi-Sab is that the truth comes from observing nature, that greatness appears in obvious but forgotten details. We can awaken that beauty with ugliness. Everything is permanent; everything crashes fades and eventually becomes nothing. All products are incomplete because nothing is perfect with the smallest details. As things wear out, they become even less accurate. All objects are unfinished, unconscious, turning or decaying. Wabi-Sabi talks about smaller, subtle and hidden details. Details invisible to the ordinary eye, which can be done with patient patience. The beauty of Wabi-Sab can be matched to what you think is ugly. The vision is dynamic; it can appear at any time, even amid ugliness.

The Wabi-Sabi spiritual state is an inevitable acceptance and appreciation of the cosmic order. A little comforting, because we know that all existence has the same fate. It is the appreciation of the cosmic order.

The moral precepts of Wabi-Sab are to get rid of all that is unnecessary and to focus on the essential which naturally belongs without disregarding the material hierarchy. It is a delicate balance between the pleasures we get from things and the joys we get from the freedom of ideas. An item receives wabi-sabi status only when it is appreciated as such. Then it disappears from existence.

The material properties of Wabi-Sab refer to a natural process, irregularities, intimacy, lack of prejudice, secularity, turbidity and simplicity. The materials will wear out during use. Wrong in the way that many consider ugly, intimate so small and something you need to approach, it is not pretentious to be understandable, mundane because it has not moved from its natural state, obscured as cloudy or muddy, only as the state of Grace arrived sober, humble. Honest intelligence.

Wabi-sabi/ Myer Fabry

The Wabi-Sabi collection reflects Japanese aesthetics and the Zen concept of finding beauty in imperfect, permanent and imperfect things. The world of Wabi-Sab contains metaphysics, spiritual values, state of mind and moral tendencies, and material qualities. Our designs represent these concepts using random patterns and clean design elements.

The Wabi-Sabi collection picks colour values mainly from nature with earthy tones such as brown, grey, black, olive green and rust, and includes colourful accents. The patterns and textures are created with an exciting selection of recycled polyester, resulting in a highly integrated collection that fits all markets.

Charade is inspired by forms and elements found in nature. A simple organic theme imitates twigs and twigs. The subtle variation of colours and stripes creates dimensions. The colour combinations are a blend of raw, olive green, tinted gold, brown and black.

Karma represents the decorative elements of Japanese decorative teapots. Versatile fabrics create a subtle contrast to the earthquake. The result is a good mid-range pattern in nine colours, from opal to obsidian.

There are countless design signs for uneven cobblestone streets. Small and beautiful circular shapes overlap with the form of a horizontal linear grid. Different types of recycled yarns create unique patterns. Soft colour combinations were distinguished from the Wabi-Sabi palette, such as brown with indigo, black with grey and fabric with blue.

Reiki is reminiscent of woven screens and rugs in Japanese tea rooms. The finely detailed pattern weaves vertical and horizontal linear strokes to create a unique, organic profile. The fresh colour combinations marry Wabi-Sab, grey and brown olives with traces of lemon, magenta and purple.

Tangled Web is an asymmetric organic design in a sophisticated combination of polyester and recycled nylon. The use of bright yarn creates a subtle contrast to the mat floor in colours such as blue, copper, olive and chalk.

The site is a beautiful blue pattern that serves as a level of coordination for Wabi-Sabi specimens, environmental, ecosphere and elemental collections. The site is characterised by horizontal ribs and occasional touches with added colour.

What is wabi-sabi, and for what reason is it hard to characterise?

Wabi-sabi is a way of life and characteristic feature of what is perceived as traditional Japanese beauty. It is difficult to define because it is never used representationally and symbolically, and also because it is a hybrid model of the subjective and objective of a blurry line, never fully realised.

How is wabi-sabi different from modernism? How is it the same?

To start, both are a radical departure/response from previous modes of art, and non-representational ideals and beauty consisting of human-made objects, spaces, and designs. What distinguishes the two are feelings, implication, location, orientation, and so much else. Wabi-Wabi is warm, generally dark and dim, present-oriented and expressed in the private domain. In contrast, modernism is fresh, usually light and bright, future-oriented, and showed in the public domain.

What is the metaphysical basis of wabi-sabi? What are its spiritual values?

The metaphysical basis of wabi-wabi is that things are devolving toward, or evolving from, nothingness; and, its spiritual values are 1. Truth originates from the perception of nature: 2. Enormity exists in the subtle and disregarded subtleties, and 3. Magnificence can be persuaded out of offensiveness.

What is the wabi-sabi state of mind? What are its moral precepts?

A wabi-sabi state of mind is one that accepts the inevitable and appreciates the cosmic order. Its moral precepts are to focus on the intrinsic, ignore material hierarchy, and to get rid of all that is unnecessary.

What are the material qualities of wabi-sabi?

The material qualities of wabi-sabi reflect natural processes and are: irregular, intimate, unpretentious, earthy, murky and straightforward. Simplicity is the core of wabi-sabi, and its nothingness is what makes it what it is. Karen writes, "The simplicity of wabi-sabi is probably best described as the state of grace arrived at by a sober, modest, heartfelt intelligence."

CHAPTER FOUR

Wabi-sabi Simplifying

Wabi-Sabi", an aesthetic design that has recently attracted the attention of interior designers and magazines, is a Japanese tradition that embraces simplicity and celebrates imperfection. Think of beautiful minimalism with a sense of character and the use of memorabilia to make a house truly a home. We have partnered with Beth Kempton, a Japanese life coach and author of Wabi-Sab, Japan: Wisdom of Japan for a Perfectly Incomplete Life to share more about this lifestyle trend and to show how it can be awakened in our homes.

Wabi-Sabi celebrates asymmetry and character and rejects the consequent novelty, uniformity and sterility. Nature itself is the ultimate inspiration. With less set of rules and more mindset, the principles of wabi-sab can be channelled into our living spaces through botanical touches that add to the feeling of tranquillity, beauty and happiness. Great houseplants remind us that the experience of being in the area is as important as how space looks.

Beth Kempton explains: "With roots in Zen and the tea ceremony, Wabi-Sabi philosophy reminds us that in nature, everything is unstable, imperfect and imperfect, so imperfection is the natural state of all things, including ourselves. This belief removes the pressure to achieve perfection. "

Understanding Beth's advice that our beautiful houseplants do not last forever, they are certainly not perfect, and instead, we learn to celebrate our own (and our plants') unique flaws.

We want to show you houseplants that reflect the wabi-sab because of their exciting shapes, their details, as you look more closely at their stems, because of the shade of new shoots and the intricate patterns of the leaves. Appreciation of all these subtleties is the essence of wabi-sab.

How does Wabi-Sabi improve simplification?

The Japanese term Wabi-Sabi is a form of understanding of the beauty of simplicity. This is an idea for many Westerners.

Wabi means no earthly "wealth" while no material things are needed. Sabin defines the feeling of loneliness and loneliness that Garr Reynolds described in Zen as "a feeling that can be when you walk alone on a deserted beach in deep contemplation."

The terms are combined for the sake of simplicity.

A story called "The Fish Story", as told in Presentation Zen, tells us that it is essential to reduce something to its primary form:

Vijay opened the store and said, "We sell fresh fish here". His father suggested removing "us" because he felt the company was more visible than the customer. The symbol was changed to "Fresh fish is sold here".

Then his brother suggested deleting the word "here" because it was clear where the fish was being sold. "Here" was a comma and the text reads "fresh fish was sold".

Her sister said that "sold" can be removed from the label because where else is it sold? The rest is 'fresh fish'.

The neighbour finally mentioned that the freshness of the fish is reflected in the fish itself.

The sign said "RIBE" when Vijay noticed the smell and appearance of his shop causing him to sell fish. Thus, in its final form, the brand became an image of a fish with the word "fresh".

"By removing the original meaning of the image, the artist can confirm it." - Scott McCloud

How close are we to Wabi-Sabu in our lives? Why?

In Western culture, grunge is famous: boundless, messy, chaotic because we believe that less is no longer. This is proof that many of us in our lives are not close to Wabi-Sabu.

It's not right in a society that sees so many messages.

As indicated by the American Marketing Association, "the normal buyer is presented to up to 10,000 brand messages a day."

What does this mean for your performance? It competes with many other messages, and most of these messages are grunge-style. Why? Because the more people think, the better.

It's nicer - as Churchill said, "I did it more than usual because I didn't have time to be shorter," but it's not better.

Simplicity can be replaced by emptiness, and while emptiness is always pure, simplicity is not yet empty.

An Ancient philosophical term

Wabi-Sabi is derived from the Japanese words "wabi", which means being alone and bothering to simplify others. And there is "Sabi" which implies the passage of time, the beauty of the passage of time.

Life can't be perfect forever, "my Japanese mother used to say on the other side of the line when I called her in a little crash in New York. Chaotic moments.

For each year I spent in the city, I began to be more open and adopt the emphatic wabi-sab.

When I was young, I recognised myself as a "mixed" or "hapa" girl (half Japanese and half Polish). The incredible immigrant parents raised me, raised me differently, felt different, and of course looked different. They disturbed me in high school from first grade, just because of the appearance.

As a former model of the fashion industry, perfection was the cornerstone of my profitability and kept me mentally on the road to "good enough" by industry standards. I have been paid to maintain a perfect look, size, waist, hips and thighs for over a decade of my career.

This "perfect" vision and should always be "positive" was and always will be unrealistic. This was entirely at odds with my Japanese education.

As a girl who struggled with heart because of failed relationships, I thought the link had to be perfect as well. I thought, what the hell did I do wrong? At that time, I could see that these incomplete calls to work later in life for subscription taxi sharks in the following steps, and I am sure that all my best friends knew that it was always the best. Wabi-Sabin through, I learned that these painful steps would bring me closer to the right people.

How can you decide to make it more comfortable in your daily life? When I studied for many years with the simplification and awareness mielenosoittajieni Kōyasan mountains and Shikoku Island in Japan, I realised it was for us.

We can practice wabi sab in honour of imperfection. Changing your mindset with this ancient practice has changed every day, whether it's a busy and uncomfortable day when I feel like everything comes to me or a peaceful, beautiful and light day wabi-sabi.

I'll let wabi-sab build my thoughts. Instead of forcing myself to practice what society considers "normal and positive" and feeling that I had to measure myself or prove myself to someone, I stopped looking for perfection. Instead, I think internally of my integrity, Wabi-Sabi. I never again want to be "manufactured by another," I'm ready.

Travelling around the world and years spent in New York have shown me rough edges and dark corners. Then I started to see my crazy everyday life in New York completely incomplete. My older sister once told me, "Candice, without darkness, there can be no light," I lived behind this.

We must learn to value all things as a whole. However, it took a long time to resolve all of this. Believe that everything is in perfect time. I hope you will see the light in the dark from my painful experiences and previous research.

Here are some ways to change your mind with wabi-sab:

Challenge yourself with nature

Changing the seasons is a great teacher for us. You can walk, walk or run and take some time to think. Watch for your walking flaws, your precious holidays in the sun, your fingers in the water, your Bunzis in the warm sand. Turn off your phone and take part in real life.

Stop the comparison

It's something we all do and is similar to wabi-sabi, and the comparison goes on and on. Commercial comparison to celebrate. Then they say, "compare is the thief of joy," and I feel a lot better when I'm weird, nerdy and quiet.

Do not compare yourself anymore, the most beautiful flowers bloom together, so start living simply, in peace with the people around you, and realise that we are all people here.

Simple

Guess what? You already have everything you need. When we ask less, spend less, buy less, we can open our hearts to too many important things. Like creating humility, character, and grace, this is a long and internal practice. But also, you have to start with something, so why not simplify your life now?

Say goodbye to vampires (people who suck your life) and see what friends celebrate and support you! Remember the physical, beauty, beautiful things and toys that you can't bring with you when you leave.

I don't care so much about it

In Japanese, we call it "shikata ga nai" (仕方が無い), so it does what my mother does. The more you are concerned about perfection and passing (Followers, Likes, comparisons), the more you will enjoy what life has to offer. It's your journey, lots of obstacles, traps, rocks, turns, turns and surprises.

It was never a perfect destination. Wouldn't an ideal life be boring? Not interested You can overcome every obstacle, but you must remember to stop autofocus.

Self-esteem your best friend

Treat yourself well; it is useful for you to relax a little and learn to worship. I have unique characteristics, which I have not always liked about myself, and I have learned to love them, they make each one of us just as we are. Whether it's a dark corner, a steep mountain or uphill, you're right where you should be. Trust yourself as a best friend and love yourself right away.

Adoption

Can we all understand that everyone is doing their best? Accepting that we all have a breakdown, you are incomplete, I have flaws, and we can change the acceptance judgment. You don't have to tell others how to live or take the exam. Remember, live and let live.

Value

My sister and I frequently talk about how beautiful the world would be if we valued character and grace, wisdom and honesty, and money, power, beauty, and social standing. Who cares about followers? Like does not measure its value.

Tell your friend how amazing they are in real life, invite them to dinner (which she will cook for you), get a new book and a little wisdom, we are students forever. Admire someone who works on a non-profit or volunteer basis to help others in real life. These are the real worthy heroes of our time, come out and start living.

Mask

For ten years of my career on the wall, I like it, my friend it's time to payback. I'm not perfect. I do not want to be. So why do I love everyone around me? Ask yourself the same and continue the course. You know, everyone wants to take off that mask, and you do, let everyone around you do the same.

Yes, girl, I still remember those dark corners, the steep mountains, the shadows cast in their visions. By following my ancestors in Japan to realise perfect relationship ideas (ideal man, mind unlikely!), Your constant positive mindset depends on my belief that perfection does not exist, but accepting that everyone is doing their best.

He would be a fool to haunt perfection and its short forms.

Remember: Perfection is dangerously transient, and if we follow it regularly, we will fool ourselves. Stay on course, notice that everyone is doing their best and enjoying your life to the fullest.

wabi-sab's philosophy has captured the interior world with natural wood furniture and bowls

A hundred years old Japanese philosophy celebrating simplicity and imperfect beauty seems to have been at home in our living spaces

From Higga, Denmark and Lagos, Sweden, we have become acquainted with other concepts that are indistinguishable from different cultures and should help us to live better.

And there is Wabi-Sabi, a little harder to open a Japanese sentence rooted in Zen Buddhism.

Put, wabi-sabi is the discovery of beauty in imperfection and imperfection, which is why the beautifully cloudy "wabi-sabi" bowls and natural wood furniture have shocked the inner world.

Which means wabi-sabi

"Wabi-Sabi has come to represent a natural and rustic side that respects flaws, organic materials, textures and characters," says Beth Kempton, a Japanese cultural expert. "I love objects with these qualities, and I decorate my home with them. But they are not wabi-sabi in the deepest sense."

Kempton, whose book Japanese Wisdom for a Complete Imperfect Life has been translated into 24 languages, claims that Wabi-Sabi is much harder to define. "Wabi-Sabi is much less of what we see and more of what we see," he says.

"Most people do not know that the Japanese do not use wabi-sab as an adjective. For example, if they describe an old and worn bowl, they are more likely to refer to its 'Sabi beauty.'

"Wabi" is roughly translated as fresh, simple, rustic and natural beauty, initially as a kind of spiritual loneliness in nature, while "Sabi" is often used to denote age-related vision. The origin of the term wabi-sabi is in the ancient Zen Buddhist approach to a modest and refined lifestyle. Philosophy began to permeate every aspect of Japanese culture, from art, architecture and poetry to design, gardening, and tea.

"It's a worldview that helps us recognise the permanent, imperfect and imperfect nature of everything, including ourselves, and inspires us to think about what it means for our lives and how we see ourselves and others," Kempton says.

Wabi-Sabi and Thoughtfulness

Wabi-Sabi's ideas also began to appear in well-being and food. Aqua Kyoto's central London restaurant currently has a philosophy-based wabi-sabi menu. A three-course meal is served in a bowl, but it also defends strange "ugly" and herbal ingredients that might otherwise be rejected for their shortcomings. The menu means diners to slow down and take in the surrounding world, and the restaurant also organises food-related workshops to complement the meal.

In the UK, Kempton has a wellness holiday with sold-out flags that incorporate the Wabi-Sabi principles and believes the modern world has a healthy appetite for the Wabi-Sabi philosophy. "We live everywhere at the moment of information. From the minute we wake up to bed, we get messages about how we should look, dress, eat and shop, the amount we ought to acquire, who we should love and how we ought to be guardians."

"We have landed at the point where we need to stop, glance around and choose for ourselves what is significant. Wabi-Sabi can help us here, which makes this hundred of years old adapting more significant than any other time in recent memory."

Worn Interiors and Trouser Bowls

If you can't stand the philosophical side of wabi-sab, and you want a comfortable and relaxing home, don't feel too guilty about your adoption. Kempton, who has spent many years studying philosophy in Japan, believes that the term wabi-sabi does nothing wrong when describing the unique, old, imperfect aspect of interior design. "It is worth it for us to have a word from a perspective that helps us to respect and cherish it."

Trouva brand creative director Lucy Ward, whose wabi-sabi collection sales increased by 53 per cent, says: Decorated with handmade home accessories with a homemade quality and an incomplete look. "

There is a wave of picturesque beautiful woodcut boards, claystone vases, beige shades, terracotta, clay and coal, and workshops to repair broken bowls with Kintsugi gold-plated technology (though in Japan you can see Kintsugi as a private boat reserved.

Heal has a Wabi-Sabi magic set of dishes in Dabia, containing bowls, plates and cups, and Kinto vases that show the growth of a broken onion.

Even the Sainsbury's trend has removed wabi-sab from its summer porcelain collection in a deep blue salad bowl with flawed edges.

How you have a Home and a Loved One

Even though he thinks Instagram is, wabi-sabi doesn't mean buying new things. In his book, Kempton describes the Wabi-Sabi home as "a place of precious things that contains love and memories, not just new things bought with impulse. It is not right or wrong. It is a simple style, executed in a perfectly imperfect way."

It is an alternative to the "exhausting" perfection of minimalism: because of one thing, you have the opportunity to be things.

Instead, according to Kempton, it is more about "mental simplicity" and nice cleavage without doing things clinically minimal.

Enough and focusing on what you can do with what is a catastrophe, even though they are catastrophes, they are more important than a large replacement budget. Wabi-Sabi's houses are, according to him, "lived, loved, and never completed."

Wabi-Sabi-Way

The word Wabi-Sabi is something you may have heard as of late on Instagram, particularly among the individuals who need to embrace a progressively direct, greener and more settled way of life. In any case, its foundations dated back to Japan in the sixteenth century.

Wabi-Sabi is a Japanese aesthetic that was born out of a reaction to the splendour and excess of time. It embraces and celebrates the beauty of imperfection, persistence, asymmetry, imperfection and simplicity while respecting nature and its processes.

The term Wabi-Sabi is not an exact translation, and it is impossible because Wabi-Sabi is more than an idea: it is a concept rooted in Japanese culture that sums up its entire worldview. But loosely translated, "Wabi" can mean rustic simplicity and serenity, and "Sabi" the beauty of old age and clothing: patina, rust and blemishes that cannot be imitated except in periods.

Wabi-Sabi is a used goods store, your grandmother's cabinets, a well-used baking tray. They are the leaves that fall in the fall, compost the leaves in the winter, the flowers that melt as smooth as snow in the spring and the lush green canopy in the summer. They are handmade objects, hand-shaped and framed with markings and asymmetry that can only be achieved with human hands. It has the scent of old leather, cracks and cracks in concrete, seats on the outside bench, paper faded in the sun and worn clothes. It is a painting made in his studio or a dried flower vase on a table, which in its current state has received a new aesthetic. Note that everything is in a state of change, and over time, everything will change.

Invest in Wabi-sabi ideale for your own home and style

You can do this without knowing what is in itself a great concept of the process of natural imperfection. Just looking around can create a different picture of things. My husband sees an old rusty jasmine fence that he thinks needs to be demolished (God forbid!). I see a great piece of history where nature works to fill the cracks and joints and, of course, to keep the fence.

Tell nature

See the shapes and shadows cast commonly. See the subtleties of the trees on earth. Make a walk back and look at the 10,000-foot view and see a few branches hanging easily and others arriving at the sky. Take a picture, Observe the branches for visible lichens or ivy, which begins to crawl around the bottom of the tree. Choose a fallen office or a piece of wood floating on the beach and appreciate its natural shape. Keep the bouquet from the date of expiration and see what happens. Remove old water! Press a few flowers between the pages of the book. Grow a small garden of plants and vegetables.

Delivery nature

In your home, according to your style. You can incorporate your branches, twigs, leaves, flowers and rocks into your household without resembling a bird's nest. A simple flower or a large leaf stem in a bottle or a handful of wavy sticks in an old ceramic base is a tight beauty because sometimes, mostly with Wabi-Sab, less is more.

Look at the houses for interested text

It is incredible what you see if you look at the close-up. Look up, look down, look down. The concrete wall outside can become the perfect backdrop for a simple style session. Those cracks on the garage floor or even the back door can add an incredible amount of interest to photography. Yes, I used pictures in both places. Weather, a worn-out substrate, a concrete strip with different patterns, an outdoor table, an oak-night table, a wooden coffee table, or even a fireplace when taken out of context and close to the small square you need for your photo. Change the look completely.

The number of times the object objects are

You don't need to be a gatherer or your house that looks like a museum. The essential thing about

Wabi-Sabi objects is that they matter to you: you are interested in them because you value the manufacturer's estimates or weather damage. Every purpose has a story. Second-hand shops, garages and recycling facilities are designed to achieve mildly rustic simplicity and subtle elegance. They are also a great place to look for items that could be wallpapered: old and rusty barbecue patterns, ripe wood board, old tablecloths and other sheets, black baking dishes, old cabinet doors. Remember to look at these things with different eyes to imagine how they can be used in a photographic context.

It stops for Recovery

Underestimated elegance and simplicity are the keywords here. When it comes to style, it sometimes means more reduction than more. Simple maintenance enhances the authenticity and silence of the settings and allows the rustic qualities of each element to pass through. The break causes a feeling of deprivation and loneliness, both of which are the hallmarks of Wabi-Sabi's ideal. Bored beauty and peace are respected when things are simplified. Applying these concepts to everyday life would change!

CHAPTER FIVE

Spiritual

Wabi-Sabi turns freely into "zen goods". Wabi-Sabi, which goes beyond our usual beauty ideas, such as flowering height, also means careful observation and recognition of beauty discretely and incompletely.
Three Spiritual Principles of Wabi-Sabi Beauty:
1. Truth comes from observing nature.
   All things are permanent, incomplete and incomplete.

2. Size is discrete and overlooked.

   We tend to forget about the smaller and the hidden, the damaged and the unstable, the quiet and short-lived, the smooth and the subtle.
3. Beauty can be distinguished from ugliness.

   Beauty is not always or just exhaustion. Beauty is a dynamic event; A great moment of poetry and grace. It often happens completely unexpectedly and spontaneously.

   Wabi-Sabi has its roots in Zen Buddhism. His philosophy and principles are presented in a tea ceremony proclaiming rituals and values of purity, simplicity, and imperfection. For example, the precious bowls of the Masters were handmade and irregular in shape, with crooked glasses and cracks, and in their intentional fault had a unique beauty.

It is believed that wabi-sabi beauty can only exist in the physical world, "in reality" like a bowl or leaf, and is not present in the image of a container or spatula. I have a different opinion. I think our brains can turn pictures into reality based on our experience of nature. Also, I believe these images will help us improve our distinction between life and between us.

Metaphysical basis

Demystifying Wabi-Sabi

Wabi-Sabi is the beauty of imperfect, permanent and imperfect things.

It is the beauty of simple and humble things.

That's the beauty of the unusual thing.

As you sit under the cherry blossoms at a typical wine party in Japan, it's easy to forget that there is a unique tribute behind an alcohol-filled celebration that focuses on embracing temporality and imperfection. Nothing endures, nothing is excellent, and nothing is perfect.

Artistic ideas are the basis for Japan's cultural identity, and Japanese have all sorts of original words to describe our perceptions of the world. Still, all of this is based on the term wabi-sabi (侘 寂).

Because it refers to the concepts of beauty, it is a term that has been understood and deliberately hidden throughout history, often by those who add mystical knowledge or objects that claim to convey Wabi-Sabi qualities. The misconception is that wabi-sabi is not a natural attribute of things, but an "event" or state of mind. In other words, wabi-sab's beauty "happens"; Do not live directly in premises or surroundings.

Definition

Wabi-Sabi, in its full expression, can be a way of life. At least it's a unique beauty.

The English word, which is mainly wabi-sabi, is probably "rustic": simple, artistic or unmarked, "but while many see an initial impression when they see the word wabi-sabi, it represents only a limited dimension to the Wabi-Sabi aesthetic of Wabi-Sabi. Sabi also has some features with "primitive art", that is, objects that are mundane, simple, unassuming, and created from natural materials.

The Japanese words "wabi" and "Sabi" originally had completely different meanings, which have blurred over the centuries so that they can be used interchangeably today.

History

Wabi-Sabi was designed and developed in Japan during the Sengoku era (ca. 1466-1598) during a period of intense political and social upheaval and is sometimes compared to the dark ages of Europe.

The invention was a tea room where artistic and philosophical values, independent of ordinary society, were rooted in isolation from the hardships and concerns of the outside world. Leaders of this creative adventure were the tea masters who prepared and presented the tea during carefully planned ceremonies, distinguished by their originality and unpredictability.

Among the historically respected tea masters was Sen no Rikyu (千 利 休):

Pre-Rikyu

The original inspiration for the wabi-sabi principle comes from the ideas of simplicity, naturalness and acceptance of reality found in Taoist and Chinese Zen Buddhism. It was also absorbed into the ethereal atmosphere of Noha, a form of Japanese musical performance known as Yugen (Deep Grace and Fineness).

By the 16th century, separate Wabi-Sabi elements had blended into the various features of sophisticated Japanese culture, reaching its zenith at the tea ceremony (茶の湯). The tea ceremony became a cultural art form, combining architecture, interior and garden design, flower arrangements, painting, cooking and exhibition.

The first wabi-sabi master was Murata Shuko (村田 珠光), Nara's Zen monk who deliberately used homemade cutlery instead of other well-decorated aliens.

Rikyu

Merchant Boy Sen no Rikyu (1522-1591) led the Wabi-sabi apotheosis in the late 16th century by placing anonymous Japanese, and Korean folk names on the same artistic level as the soft Chinese treasures Carry the meaning and significance of physical objects, environment and events. A new type of tea room was created, based on the shape of a farmhouse made of coarse mud walls, thatched ceilings and erroneous removal of beams. Exposed tree.

By consciously combining the old with the new, smooth, coarse, precious, expensive, for example, simple, old grated rice bowls, you could love to repair and put them in teacups. In other words, images of pagan poverty were actively cultivated.

His wealthy employer did not appreciate his aesthetic ideals and ordered Rikki to perform rituals at the age of seventy.

Post-rikyu

Like religious fundamentalists who claim that their interpretation of the doctrine was "correct," organised tea groups were concerned about reaffirming their legitimacy based on Rikyu's teachings after his death. In the process, personal judgment and imagination were squeezed out of the ceremony, even the most famous gestures were written by hand. This has led to the institutionalised wabi-sab becoming the opposite: elegant, bright and abundant, despite maintaining the uniformity of traditional forms.

Wabi-Sabi is no longer just the ideological or spiritual heart of tea, although the things that sound and look like wabi-sab are still exposed to the orthodoxy of tea.

Hiding certain movements

Although almost all Japanese claim to understand the Wabi-Sabi feeling, it should still be one of the main concepts of Japanese culture, and few can express that feeling.

Most Japanese have never learned intellectually about wabi-sab because there are no books or teachers about it. This is no accident. Throughout history, a reasonable understanding of wabi-sab has been deliberately denied:

Zen Buddhism: Wabi-Sabi is associated peripherally with Zen Buddhism as an example of many of the most essential spiritual, philosophical principles of Zen. In Zen science, necessary information can only be transmitted through the mind to the mind, not through the written or spoken word. "Those who know do not say; those who know do not know." As a result, a clear definition was carefully avoided.

Iemoto System: Japanese cultural arts, such as tea ceremony, floral arrangements, calligraphy, singing and dance, are traditionally controlled by family business groups led by nimotoiemoto (家 元). Information on "exotic" terms such as wabi-sabi is often artistically disguised as a bait marketing tool used to attract potential customers.

Beautiful blur: the myth of unhappiness with wabi-sab is appreciated because, according to some Japanese critics, inaccuracy is part of its uniqueness. From this perspective, the lack of intact information is simply another aspect of wabi-sabi imperfection. A full explanation of the concept could reduce it.

The Wabi-Sabi universe

Wabi-Sabi can be called an "integral" aesthetic system. His vision of the world, that is, the universe, is self-referential. It provides an integrated approach to the finite nature of existence (metaphysics), sacred knowledge (spirituality), emotional well-being (mental state), behaviour (morality), object appearance and emotion (materiality). The more systematically and clearly defined the components of an aesthetic system, the more useful it will be.

Metaphysical Foundations

Things evolve or evolve from scratch, p. E.g. Wabi-Sabi, in its purest form, speaks of these delicate traces on the verge of stupidity. Instead of space, as in the West, there is a gap with potential.

Spiritual value

As of late, I discovered that wabi-sabi isn't just tasteful, yet also, a way of thinking conceived of a Japanese world-see dependent on Taoism and impacted by Zen Buddhism. In Taoist cosmology, it is accepted that all things appearing in the world come from the vast emptiness known as Tao, and eventually everything returns to Tao. We are all part of a connected life system, and everything is in a state of constant change.

Over time, new things come, and old things go. Nature dances over time and allows us to appreciate its beauty over time as it changes its physical appearance. Wabi-Sabi's philosophy and aesthetics are derived from observing nature and have been cultivated and supplemented by most Japanese cultures for hundreds of years. The word "wabi" was initially used to describe the lonely lifestyle of a monk who renounced all his worldly possessions for a simple, disciplined life. Today it stands for rustic simplicity, tranquillity, attention to detail and unobtrusive beauty. "Sabi" is used to denote desertification and desert, such as reed after frost. It is related to the idea that every sensitive being dies with time. Today it is used to express the physical beauty that is revealed when an object begins to look its age. A thirteenth-century Zen monk combined these two words to describe aesthetic philosophy resulting from his humble efforts to express his love for a balanced life amid the inability of life. The Wabi-Sabi aesthetic transcends conventional beauty and seeks to evoke deeper emotions within us, in harmony with our intuition and early childhood experiences.

In the Zen tradition, we experience true beauty when we allow ourselves to be curious and open to change and approach life without judgment. The vision is not dominant or formulated. The Wabi-Sabi aesthetic is rooted in Japanese culture and is an example of tea art where every detail is carefully considered. By participating in beauty through a work of art, we can deepen our understanding, connection, and respect for our lives. Wabi-sab is always approached with humility and sincerity. He is humble, imperfect and unclean. It has defective features of nature and humanity and the colours of autumn. Enjoy the moment and highlight the beauty of old age in the physical world, which mirrors the irreversible progression of life in the profound domain.

The truth comes from observing nature.

All things are immutable to planets and stars, and even intangible things like family heritage, historical memory, scientific statements, great art and literature eventually forget and do not exist.

Everything is incomplete, even the sharp edge of the enlarged razor blade reveals microscopic wells and saws. As things begin to crumble, they become even less perfect and uneven.

All things are incomplete, including the universe itself, and are in a state of continuous formation or disintegration. The concept of maturity is not based on wabi sab.

"Majesty" appears as discrete and overlooked details, unlike the western idea of beauty, because it is something monumental, spectacular and lasting, wabi-sabi is not a moment of flowering and abundance, but moments of explosion or looseness. It is remote and hidden, litigation and short-lived: things are so subtle and empty that they are invisible to the eyes. To encounter wabi-sabi, you have to back off, be persistent and pay special attention.

Beauty can be combined with ugliness: wabi-sabi suggests that vision is a dynamic event that takes place between you and the rest. This can happen at any time, given the right circumstances, context or perspective. Although the peasant cabin is in a shallow environment, in the right and guided environment, you can obtain extraordinary beauty.

CHAPTER SIX

Soul Nurturing

We live in a time algorithm to hack the brain, pop-up propaganda and information everywhere. As soon as we wake up in bed, they send us messages about how we should see, dress, eat and buy, how much we should earn, who we should love and how we should give birth. Many of us are likely to spend more time thinking about other people's lives than investing alone. Add to this momentum that encourages us to act, and it is not surprising that many of us feel exhausted, insecure, liberated, and exhausted. Also, we are surrounded by bright artificial light at home, in the shop and office, on phones and laptops. We are too tall and obsessed with productivity. It destroys our nervous system and our ability to sleep.

We pay the price for projecting a relaxing shadow and creamy texture of our lives for speed and efficiency. Our eyes and hearts are tired. Although powerful and valuable, social networks make us dependent on comparison and dependencies for validation. We pause precious moments of our lives for taking and preparing photographs, and at that point spend the following hour checking how much endorsement we have gotten from individuals we scarcely know. Every time we have free minutes, the phone turns off, and we turn our eyes as we move into another person's beautiful life, jealous jealousy, because we assume they live that way. Every time we do this, we lose the unknown opportunities for communication, tranquillity, and daily adventure in our lives because the mind has gone somewhere, the body cannot follow it.

Few of us can move on without forcing what others think. We sit in a row waiting for someone else's permission as we worry about things that haven't happened yet. We talk about our limits to ourselves, weakening where we measure and paying more where we fall.

And here's the real irony. What we look for outside is often different from what we want inside. We have reached at the point where we have to pause, look around and decide for ourselves what is important. Wabi-Sabi can help us here, which makes this celebration of learning more relevant than ever today.

A new way

We now need a new way of seeing the world and our place in it. We need new approaches to the challenges of life. We need tools for conscious and conscious living and a framework for deciding what matters to us so that we can transcend our constant desire for more, better and better. We need to find ways to reduce speed so that life does not rush side by side.

We need to begin to notice more beauty to lift our spirits and stay inspired. We must allow ourselves to enjoy judgment and the endless quest for perfection. And we must begin to see for ourselves and ourselves the perfect imperfect treasure of what we are.

Everything we so desperately need is found in wabi-sab's philosophy. Not because it solves cosmetic problems, but because it can, in principle, change the way we see life. Wabi-Sabi teaches us to be less satisfied in a way that looks more:

- Fewer things, more soul. Less hurry, more ease. Less chaos, calmer.

- Less mass consumption, more unique creation.

- Less complexity, more clarity. Less evaluation, more forgiveness.

- Less harassment, more truth.

- Less resistor, higher resistor. Less control, more surrender.

- Less head, more heart.

Wabi-Sabi is a precious layer of wisdom that values peace, harmony, beauty, and imperfection, and can strengthen our resistance to modern evils. It is also essential that accepting imperfection does not mean lower standards or giving up life. It means not judging yourself for what it is: completely imperfect, both unique to you and us all. Put it on, and wabi-sabi lets you be alone. He encourages him to do his best but does not seem sick without reaching the goal of inaccessibility. It makes you relax, slow down and enjoy life. And it shows that beauty is found in the most incredible places, which makes the daily door a joy.

How to inspire touch shopping

How do you look at the excess and the waste in a spiralling and toxic reference culture and decide to do things differently? How can you be a defender of something that feels more real?

The most emotional purchase of all is the one that costs nothing and adds only what you have to your natural beauty. Try spending time in the wild, collecting gifts from the woods, or creating hands instead of shopping. When considering buying a new one, ask yourself:

- Do I need it? Already have something that can do this job? Am I going to use it?

- Do you love her? Do you still want it in 24 hours? Now for a year? The longing contains beauty. Can I wait a moment to be sure?

- Will it be useful during my current life (or will I buy it, will I try to hold on to the past, or carry on a specific version of my life in the future)?

- Does it work with other things?

- Will you help me use the space more flexibly?

- Is this something you can get for free when borrowing or exchanging?

- What I am prepared to deal with, so I could make room for this?

- What do I have to sacrifice to pay for it? Is it worth it?

- Is it made from natural materials? If not, is there a version?

- Is it worth paying a little more to get a durable version?

Principles for wabi-sab

Below is a summary of my ten fundamental principles for a wabi-sabi-inspired home. While wabi-sabi-Esque objects should play a role, they are not the perfect picture. Here is a guide to the philosophy of wabi-sab. It's great that your home is up and running. Real-life is not like design magazines.

You have to live in the house, so you don't have to wait until everything is over before inviting your friends to enjoy being together.

1. Use your mark, which is called Genkan in Japan. Order out-of-season jackets. Take off the flowers. Ask visitors to leave Japanese-style shoes at the door (and try to encourage everyone who lives with you to change their habit). Put your shoes on shelves or in a shoebox or maybe under the stairs. You may want to provide guests with slippers for your home if the floor is cold. This keeps it clean everywhere and gives you an immediate sense of comfort and familiarity.

2. Cleaning saves you time and money and lets you appreciate the things you love. However, absolute minimalism is another type of perfection. Instead, touch simplicity. Think clean, clean and comfortable.

3. Try natural home mats such as wood, clay and stone, and natural fabrics for linen, clothing and kitchenware. See how they bring character and tranquillity. The eye and imagination love imperfection, asymmetry and uneven surfaces.

4. Think of how true nature can bring flowers, branches, logs, feathers, leaves, shells, rocks,

handmade canopies, basketballs, etc. into your space.

5. Consider both light and shadow and observe how contrast changes its state at different times of the day. Embrace the twilight and darkness as it suits your season and mood.

6. Think about the five senses of your space. It depends on your residence and type of situation. Still, it can include anything from opening a wind window to using textured fabrics in your furniture, applying essential oils to playing relaxing music. You can even consider the taste of aromas, such as using fruits and vegetables on simple screens or adding details to make your breakfast table special.

7. Deal with the things you value that adorn the space and cherish it with stories and memories. Think of opposites: past and present, foundation and inspiration, ordinary and unusual. Always be creative with what you have or reuse objects that have a past life.

8. Consider the importance of relationships and visual harmony. How do things look and feel about other items in the room and space itself? What do interior windows and doors frame? What is insight, and what is partially hidden,

implying something outside? Which different textures bring character and warmth to space?

9. Create small angles of beauty in unexpected places. Small vase in the window. A handwritten note in the bathroom. Picture framed under a pillar.

10. Observe how you need to use the space differently depending on the season and the season.

Ways to build flexibility

1. Improve your physical vitality by moving, feeding, and resting.

2. Increase your mental vitality with a peaceful, adequate sleep and a period of wildlife.

3. Practice handling small things to handle big things better.

4. Set a set of small goals and work with them.

5. Cultivate something. Pay attention to the difference in your care.

6. Track the things you do regularly to remind you how capable you are.

7. Find a community and create a support network.

8. Find and learn about flexibility models.

9. Surround yourself with inspirational offers.

10. Find reasons to be positive every day

Questions to help you adapt to nature.

Regardless of the time of year, no matter where you are in the world, you can use the instructions below to see what is happening in your neighbourhood. Try to use all your senses and look for details. If you go back here for over a year, you will discover how observing the seasons can change the manner in which you see the world.

1. What is the weather like? Pay attention to the water, wind, sun and any special conditions that apply to your location.

2. What is Light?

3. What does the night sky look like?

4. What plants and flowers are formed? Bloom? Pale? Hide?

5. What animals have you noticed lately?

6. What are the ingredients of the season today?

7. What have you been using outside lately?

8. What seasonal colours have you noticed lately?

9. What seasonal sounds have you noticed lately?

10. What seasonal flavours have you noticed lately?

11. What seasonal patterns have you noticed lately?

12. How do you feel? What is your mood?

13. How is your health? What are your energy levels?

14. What personal care should I do now? How can you exclude a season?

15. What traditions or worship have you had recently?

16. Dig in. What nature or seasonal traditions do you have in your home or community? How can you now incorporate part of the culture into your life?

17. How could you mark this season smoothly?

See the beauty in imperfection

When making a series of handmade pots, the ceramic machine would not strive for perfection in terms of symmetry and smoothness, or else they would use the device. They strive for natural beauty, hand sign and heart infusion. We didn't have to be flawless and cohesive as if we were leaving the people's factory. What would happen if you imagined yourself to be a beautiful handmade pot carefully designed and appreciated for your lack? What if you acknowledge that the structure, character and depth lie behind your natural beauty, inside and out? What if you know how everything that made you what you are today?

Over the years, we glue layers of our natural beauty in an endless quest for perfection with anti-ageing creams, accumulated items, professional titles, and projected images that we believe can enhance others than us. But everything is heavy and hides what is inside. Only when you remove the layers will you let your inner beauty shine. What would happen if we agreed that our ideal state was truly complete imperfection and that we were already there? No more fighting or exhausting the crowds. Instead, relax knowing we are as good as we are.

Going a step further, we can see how these shortcomings could be the door to new learning opportunities, experiences, discussions and contacts. Suddenly, perfect does not seem so desirable in the end, and we realise we are capable of more than we ever imagined.

Wabi-Sabi talks about things naturally and authentically. How is your 'natural and more authentic space'? Is this how you walk the world? If not, what do you need to remove to return?

CHAPTER SEVEN

State of Mind

Wabi-Sabi is a Japanese expression that is now and then hard to see, yet its consistent uncertainty is a piece of its importance and has a lot to do with lack. In human life, everything is transient, temporary and incomplete. Nothing is perfect. Many scientific truths are subjective and lack measures that could measure their perfection. People who strive for one another in their quest for perfection are always disturbed because of their desire to be perfect for attaching and carrying them. The people around him are also in love because the goal itself is biased. The perfection seekers suffer from stress, which often causes a catastrophe in their relationship.

Any purpose or purpose created by the creative mind is perfect for the person who does what it is. Others may find some flaws in it. But the person who creates something stops when the instinct calls him to stop. You feel satisfied and not enough; It should look perfect to others. Aesthetic beauty is modest and unpretentious. For example, Mona Lisa, probably the most famous painting in the world, perhaps a work of art, may not be perfect and is still considered unparalleled. The background of the picture is boring. During the same period, there were many other portraits with equally enigmatic expressions. Unnecessary focus on this image and the popularity of many other works prevent most people from seeing the picture as it is. It seems that Leonardo DaVinci, the creator of Mona Line, did not consider his excellent work.

Historical pianist Daniel Steibelt is known for challenging Beethoven for technical defects in some of his masterpieces. They even had an improvisation competition in Vienna. Steibelt lost the battle with Beethoven, but there is evidence that Steibelt was also a prolific composer. No invention, creation, art or strategy can be called into question for its soundness. Some critics find some or other bugs in it. Each individual has a different aesthetic perception. In traditional Japanese artistic thinking, they believe in accepting imperfection called wabi-sab.

The term consists of two words. First of all, wabi means that anything that looks beautiful is spotless and nonsense; Wabi explains Kintsugi, an example of bronze, ceramic statues and sculptures in heritage buildings, with special varnish mixed with gold, silver or platinum. The technology behind this is to recognise the history of the article and visibly incorporate the correction into the new paragraph rather than hiding it. The process usually produces something more beautiful than the original. I knew the other word refers to the beauty that comes with maturity, as with ancient art, structures look appealing due to slow changes. They become a symbol of philosophy, culture and history. Even people look more attractive through life experience, and wisdom gained.

Wabi-Sabi is a Japanese philosophy that nothing is permanent, nothing is perfect, and nothing is perfect. Therefore, every experience, every creation, has its beauty. All things considered, excellence is entirely subjective. What looks good on my eyes may not look right on someone else's eyes. The term wabi-sabi implies that life itself is full of qualities such as persistence, modesty, invisibility and imperfection.

Practising Wabi-Sab in your life does not involve money, qualifications, fame, space, education or special skills. All you need is a genuine feeling of serenity to appreciate the beauty; the desire to accept things as they are. It requires the ability to reduce speed, to change the balance of understanding into understanding, not to supplement something. We always hope that others are perfect without losing sight of the flaws. Nothing is ideal in the world except the word "perfect". Each has its uniqueness; Universal energy did not intentionally create a spotless world. There is no right or wrong. Accept wabi-sabi as a state of mind and live a comfortable life.

State of Mind Guide

Wabi-Sabi forces us to consider our mortality as it will inevitably be accepted, as the ruins of a brilliant castle that collapses and is enriched with weeds. This is mixed with the bitter enjoyment that all existence has in the same fate. This can evoke poetry or familiar noises that refer to sad but beautiful Wabi-Sabi feelings. e.g., the hum of the crow's sad, or the pitiful cries of the hummus.

An appreciation of the cosmic order, as well as the medieval cathedral in Europe, was built with the emotion of evoking a Transcendental feeling, the way rice paper transmits light in diffused light or how clay breaks dry represents all physical forces and deep structures. That is behind the everyday world.

Around without flowers in bloom

No maple leaves without shine,
The lonely fishing cabin itself
At dusk
This fall eve.
Moral regulations

Get rid of all that is unnecessary, and wabi-sabi means stepping on the planet and knowing how to appreciate whatever it is, irrelevant. It tells us to stop caring for success, wealth, position, strength and luxury and to enjoy a free life. This involves some difficult decisions and recognition that it is so important to know when to make decisions and when not to make decisions: let things be. We are still living in a world of ideas, and we must strike a delicate balance between their enjoyment and their enjoyment of freedom of affairs.

Focus on the internal hierarchy and ignore the symbolic bending or crawling to deliberately enter the tea room through a low and low entrance that evokes humility in an egalitarian atmosphere. Hierarchical thinking "this is higher / better, lower / worse" cannot be accepted. They are all equal. The manufacturer does not value tea room items either, or the cost of mud, paper and bamboo has more wabi-sabi properties than gold, silver and diamonds. An object only receives wabi-sabi status when it is appreciated as such.

Material quality

Natural process suggestion: Wabi-Sabi cases are expressions of the frozen time. They are made from materials that are visibly sensitive to weather and human health. They capture the language of sun, wind, rain, heat and cold, rust, discolouration, discolouration, deformation, shrinkage, drying and cracking. Although things in the wabi sab may soon be intangible (or materialised), very weak, brittle or dried, their balance and strength are still unbalanced.

The occasional wabi-sabi things are indifferent to the usual good taste. As a result, stuff with wabi-sabi often seem strange, malformed, uncomfortable, or something that many consider being silly (for example, a broken tank again).

Wabi-Sabi's intimate things are usually small and compact, quiet and internally oriented. They mean access, touch, relationship. Wabi-Sabi sites are small, secluded and private environments that enhance the ability to think metaphysically. Tea rooms often have low ceilings, small windows, small entrances and very dim lighting. They are calm and relaxing, round and reminiscent of the spot. They are a separate world: nowhere, anywhere, everywhere. Each object on the inside seems to grow inversely with its actual size.

Modest: Wabi-Sabi issues are not studied and have an inevitable aspect. They demand that they be the centre of attention. They are subtle and unassuming, but now without the presence or stupid authority. Wabi-Sabi things co-occur with the rest of the environment and are only appreciated during direct contact and use. They do not need origin; It is better if the author does not make any difference, is invisible or unknown.

The wabi-sabi things on Earth may seem crude and unclean. They are usually made of materials that are not far from the original space and have a rich raw structure and a rough feel. You may not be able to distinguish your art.

Wabi-Sabi's dark things have a vague, blurry or diminished quality because they don't happen when nothing gets close (or left). There are endless grey, brown, muted greens and whites for Wabi-Sabie.

Straightforward: effortlessness is at the core of all things wabi-sabi. Nothing is straightforward, but before and after they are not that simple. The paraphrase of Rikyo, the wabi-sabi essence expressed in tea, is simplicity itself: freshwater, gathering wood for cooking, boiling water, making tea and serving others. Further details are contained in the invention but must be limited and avoided with strict savings. Wabi-Sabi material is emotionally warm, never cold. This is achieved by:

Disrupts the core, but without removing the poetry.
Keep things clean and tidy, but not sterilised.
Keep visible functions to a minimum
Use of a limited selection of materials
Comparison with modernism

"Modernism" is another complex term that goes far beyond the history, attitudes and philosophy of art and design, but can serve as a useful reference in 21st-century industrial society to compare what is wabi-sabi and what is not (think the types you see in MoMA).

Similarities

Both apply to all kinds of human spaces, spaces and models.

Both are potent reactions to the dominant and established sentiments of their time (19th-century classicism modernism, 17th-century Wabi-Sabi Chinese perfectionism)

Both are easy to recognise surface features (modernism is sleek, bright and stylish, wabi-sabi is down to earth, imperfect and versatile)

Both remove all ornaments that are not an integral part of the structure.

Both are abstract ideals, do not represent beauty.
Differences
wabi-sabi-modernism
Expressed in Public Area Expressed in Private Area
Mass-produced / modular single / variable
Express your faith in progress No progress
Future-oriented to the present

Geometric shape (sharp, precise and defined shapes and edges)

Organic form (soft and non-dispersible forms and edges)
Human materials Natural materials
Allegedly soft supposedly raw

It must be in order. It is equivalent to degeneration and degeneration.

General light and light are usually dark and dim.

Functionality and usefulness are important values Operations and service are less important.

The Eternal
The season is the season.

Beauty is Empty

Wabi-Sabi is the antithesis of the traditional Western beauty idea, complete, permanent and Wabi-Sabi is a Japanese expression for discovering excellence in aesthetically pleasing, seamless and mass-marketed products represent, like the latest iPhone.

We often tacitly define beauty as physical perfection. But buried somewhere in our psyche is the realisation that man is fundamentally imperfect. So, when it is suggested that imperfection can be as beautiful and valuable as perfection, it is a welcome acknowledgement.

What are the doctrines of the universe?

All things are permanent.
All products are incomplete.
All products are defective.

The simplicity of Wabi-Sab is probably best described as a state of grace that comes from inadequate, humble, and cordial intelligence. The primary strategy for this intelligence is the media economy. Money for the essence, but don't remove the poetry. Keep things clean and tidy, but don't sterilise them. (Wabi-Sab's things are mentally warm, never cold.) Usually, this means a limited range of materials. It also means that significant features are minimised. But this does not mean removing the invisible connective tissue that links the elements to some meaningful entity. Nor does one's "curiosity" diminish in any way; quality forces us to look at it again and again.

Highlights

wabi refers to:
lifestyle, spiritual path
internal, subjective
philosophical construction
special events
Sabi refers to:
material subjects, art and literature
external, objective
aesthetic ideal
temporary exhibitions
Similarities between Modernism and Wabi-Sab:

Both apply to objects of all kinds, spaces and artificial patterns.

Botha reacted again to the established, established feelings of her time. Modernism was a fundamental starting point for 19th-century classicism and eclecticism. Wabi-Sabi was an essential starting point for the perfection and beauty of China in the 16th and previous centuries.

Both avoid decoration that is not an integral part of the structure.

They are both abstract ideals, not representing beauty.

Both make it easy to identify surface properties. Modernism is perfect, polished and elegant. Wabi-Sabi is down to earth, imperfect and diverse.

Differences between Modernism and Wabi-Sab

Modernism:
Mostly expressed in public domain
it represents a logical and rational view of the world
absolute
look for global and prototype solutions
Series / Modular
Express your faith in advancement
Future-oriented
Believe in nature's control.

Romance technology
People who adapt to machines.
Geometric Arrangement of Shapes (Sharp, Accurate and Defined Shapes and Edges)
Box as a metaphor (rectangular, accurate, included)
The human-made the materials
Allegedly slippery
should be fine
purity enriches expression
requests a reduction in sensory information
He tolerates ambiguities and contradictions.
Guay
Usually light and light
Function and utility are paramount values
Perfect materiality is ideal.
eternal
Wabi-Sabi:
Mostly expressed in a private area
It means an intuitive view of the world
relative
Find personal and original solutions.
Unique in type / variable
No progress
Current oriented
Believe in the inherent uncontrollability of nature.
Romance in nature
People who adapt to the landscape
Organic shape organisation (soft and undefined shapes and edges)
Bowl as a Metaphor (Free Form, Open at the Top)
Natural materials

Allegedly raw
It adapts to degradation and wears
Corrosion and pollution enrich its expression.
Ask for a sensory extension.
Feel comfortable with ambiguities and contradictions.
Warm
Usually dark and gloomy
Action and utility are not that important
Total immunity is ideal.
Everything has a season
The Wabi-Sabi universe
Metaphysical Basis: Things turn or develop from scratch
Spiritual Values:
The truth comes from observing nature.
"Size" is a separate and forgotten detail
Beauty can be distinguished from the ugliness
State of mind:
Acceptance of the inevitable
Critique in the cosmic order.
Moral Recipes:
Get rid of all that is unnecessary
Focus on the internal and ignore the material hierarchy
Material quality:
Proposal of the natural process.
irregular
intimate
Not demanding
Clay-
cloudy
easy

Wabi-Sabi to everyone

Wabi-Sabi is not just for artists, designers, poets and philosophers, but for everyone.

Anyway, here is an answer to some of the questions you were asked in the assignment.

What is wabi-sabi, and for what reason is it hard to characterise? Wabi-Sabi is felt at the core of Japanese culture. It is hard to characterize, basically in light of the fact that it stays away from the same and intellectual understanding. Japanese critics' view, it is crucial to maintain a particular mystery and complicated, which is related to the lack of aesthetic concerns "ideological clarity or transparency", which is not required wabi-Sabi. The subtleties of Japanese and the evolving meanings of the words wabi and sabi also prevent the word from being translated. Now words are almost always used together.

Just uses the word "rustic" as an English word, which is closest to Wabi-sabi, explaining that it has the characteristics of "primitive art" and secular, modest and direct.

How does wabi-sabi differ from modernism? How is it the same?

Wabi-Sabi and modernism apply to all human-made objects, spaces, and models, both of which were distinct movements of the aesthetics of his time. The extra elements of the structure do not matter: both principles are concerned with the abstract representation of beauty according to its aesthetic principles, which are quite different. While modernism is neat, polished and accurate, wabi-sabi is imperfect, imperfect and down to earth. The differences between them are similar in many ways. Some of the others that Root's book mentions are:

What is the metaphysical basis of wabi-sab? What are your spiritual values?

Wabi-Sabi's metaphysical foundation is that things are in a state of eternal return or evolution from emptiness, which, unlike Western philosophies, "lives where possible." The purest type of Wabi-Sab is attached to what Exactly calls "weak evidence" of deformation and formation. The formless inability to distinguish is also recognised in wabi-sab's aesthetics: "Unless we knew otherwise, we could confuse a newborn baby, a small, wrinkled, folded, slightly grotesque, old man at death" (Koren, p. 45).

The spiritual values of Wabi-Sab result from the perception of nature and include the acceptance of unpredictability, imperfection and incompleteness. The beauty is not significant or monumental, and it is small details, hidden and exquisite. Wabi-Sabi, on the other hand, does not distinguish between beauty and ugliness. As Koren explains, "Wabi-Sabi suggests that beauty is a dynamic event that takes place between you and someone else." And that is why beauty can appear at any time.

What is the Wabi-Sabi state of mind? What are your moral rules?

Wabi-Sabi expressions make us aware and comfortable about the inevitable aspects of nature and life. When they think of our mortality and all that surrounds us, "they awaken to existential loneliness and tender sorrow." Just use the words "bitterness of pleasure". The cosmic order of things and the intuitive nature of the world and ourselves are valued.

The moral precepts of Wabi-Sab are primarily based on the concept of "material poverty, spiritual wealth" and decisions that strike a balance between "enjoyment of things and enjoyment of freedom of things." Just uses the design of the wabi-sab tea room an example of how he values natural attribute and avoids hierarchy. In the Tea Room, everyone is forced to crawl through a small entrance, walk practically on the same level, and enter an environment where everyone is equal.

What are the material properties of wabi-sab?

The material properties of Wabi-Sab are subject to proposals from a natural process. As "vulnerable" materials, they are susceptible to natural and human-made deformation, cracks and other effects. As such, they are also irregular and do not fit into the rules of beauty. Wabi-Sabi things, as I just describe, are too intimate and separate worlds (i.e. Tea Room), modest (coexist with the environment and not found in museums), down to earth (rich and crude textures), cloudy (blurry and not approachable)) is nothing) and pure ("it diminishes materially but does not eliminate poetry").

Japanese aesthetics standard and simplicity

Although the term wabi-sabi is unknown to many Japanese, the ability to find beauty in simple, irregular and imperfect objects is an integral part of Japanese culture. According to Pilar Viladas' 2005 version of the New York Times of Root Book, wabi-sabi "spends a world of secularity, coincidence, modesty and intimacy. It is not about perfection, softness, mass production or fairy tales.", derived from our Greek and Roman heritage (monumentality, symmetry and perfection) and the reality of modern consumer culture (fame, price and trends).

According to Root, the metaphysical basis of wabi-sab is the reality of change and permanence: "things change or evolve from scratch". The fundamental values are: "The truth comes from observing nature. Greatness is present in discrete and forgotten details. Beauty can be extinguished by ugliness."

Objects that reflect the aesthetics of wabi-sab are, according to Root, "irregular; intimate; modest; earthy; dark; simple." In other words, they reflect the processes of nature and the cycle of life and death. We can find beauty in rustic simplicity, imperfection and change, and even in the processes of torsion and decay.

Historically, wabi-sabi has been associated with Zen philosophy, teaming, Japanese garden design, haiku and ikeban.

In the Japanese garden of Seattle, wabi-sabi is most evident in the kettle, the shoese, which means the shadow of the crumbling pines, which is the Roji Garden, literally a land or a road covered with dew. The green shades of the buildings, the rocks, the rustic architecture reveal the woman's emphasis on inner simplicity, humility, silence, and sharing with other types of tea.

What is wabi-sabi, and for what reason is it hard to characterise?

Wabi-Sabi is a Japanese wonder stylish that spotlights on the imperfect, imperfect and transient interior of an object.

How is wabi-sabi different from modernism? How is it the same?

According to Root, Wabi-Sabi and Modernism are healthy reactions to the dominant and settled feelings of their time, which can be applied to all kinds of artificial objects, spaces and models. However, some key differences are different:

Wabi-Sabi: Expressed in a private area, it is based on an intuitive worldview and explores the nature and organic aspects of things and solves problems with a more personalised, unique solution.

Modernism: Publicly expressed, based on a logical and rational view of the world, seeks geometric organisation of shape and solves problems with universal and prototypical solutions.

What is the metaphysical basis of wabi-sab? What are your spiritual values?

Wabi-Sabi's metaphysical foundation means that things turn or evolve toward nothing. His spiritual values include: (1) the truth comes from observing nature; (2) "greatness" appears in discrete and neglected details, and (3) beauty can be distinguished from ugliness.

What is the Wabi-Sabi state of mind? What are your moral rules?

The Wabi-Sabi spiritual state means acceptance of the inevitable and appreciation of the cosmic order. His moral commands include getting rid of unnecessary, focusing on the inner, and neglecting the material hierarchy.

What are the material properties of wabi-sab?

Wabi-sab is characterised by these material qualities: suggesting a natural process, irregularity, intimacy, lack of prejudice, secularity, darkness/vagueness and simplicity. Wabi-Sabi celebrates flaws in nature and helps us see imperfect details as things that could also be worthy of beauty.

The beauty of wabi sabi

Identifying the substrate of the wabi-sabi idea was a reflective exercise of induction and reasoning. However, I felt that the concepts that finally emerged were useful and precise. For example:

* On the metaphysical level of Wabi-Sab, beauty is on the verge of emptiness. That is the beauty that happens when things become empty. That is why wabi-sabi things are subtle and nuanced.

* The beauty of Wabi-Sab is an "event", an atmosphere, not a natural attribute of things. In other words, the "happening" beauty wabi-sabi does not live in objects and surroundings. Similarly, if you fall in love with someone or say something to a physically unattractive person, to a place or something later, you will see someone or something beautiful (at least for a moment), even if the rest of the world does not.

* Wabi sab has a compelling pedagogical dimension. Because wabi-sabi cases reveal "fair" natural processes such as ageing, imperfections, decomposition, etc., graphically reflect the existence of our mortal journeys. Therefore, the interaction with wabi-sabi objects and the environment will inevitably lead us to a more gentle acceptance of our existential destiny.

* Wabi-Sabi is the basis of the aesthetics of poverty, even though it elegantly made poverty. As such, wabi-sabi is a democratic beauty accessible to the rich and the poor.

* Wabi-Sabi is the counterpoint to the beauty of the classical, complete, permanent and monumental western idea. As such, wabi-sabi is the definite inverse of aesthetically pleasing, perfect and mass-marketed products, such as the latest portable wireless digital devices.

This last point has proved particularly resonant for many readers of my book. Perfection is one of the most essential values of our culture. We often calmly define beauty as physical perfection. But buried somewhere in our psyche is the understanding that being human is being imperfect. So, when it is suggested that imperfection can be as beautiful and precious as perfection, it is welcome recognition.

On a metaphysical level, wabi-sabi is beauty on the edge of emptiness. That is the beauty that happens when things become empty.

In everything I've had so far, there is only one small problem. Although "wabi-sabi" seems to be a Japanese term, if you look at the Japanese dictionary "wabi-sabi", you will not find it.

"Wabi" and "Sabi" have since quite a while ago existed in Japanese culture, however as isolated terms. "Sabi" is old. It is in the first anthology of Japanese poetry, compiled in the eighth century. At that time, "Sabi" meant "to be empty."

In the twelfth century, "sabi" had become an important ideal and critical concept of Japanese poetry. "Sabi" meant "to enjoy the old, faded and lonely." He also referred to the "beauty of the dry product."

Almost four hundred years later, at the end of the 16th century, "wabi" appeared to describe the new aesthetic sensibility that had just begun to be used in a tea ceremony. Over the next hundred years, "wabi" will be very modern.

During this one hundred year period, the importance of the wab will be extended; "wabi" even contains all the definitions of "sabi". The seminal moment of the theme "wabi" is the use of a term similar to Sabi to describe new "wabi" objects and environments.

Then, since the mid-seventeenth century, wabi ceased to be fashionable.

In the mid-twentieth century, some scholars used the term "wabi", while others used "Sabi" to describe primarily the same. Some researchers use both heads interchangeably. I have never found a satisfactory explanation other than the fact that, for many historical reasons, the Japanese were always in the mood with semantic ambiguity and ambiguity.

Today, if you ask an educated Japanese if he knows what "wabi-sabi" means, he answers "yes" tremendously. If you ask them to define "wabi-sabi," they probably won't be able to do it.

Despite the enormous conceptual breadth of wabi-sab, the playful adoption of various ideas and material manifestations seems to satisfy legitimate artistic, spiritual and philosophical needs. To date, dozens of other authors have written books that cite and combine the main elements of my paradigm with the word "wabi-sabi."

And although "wabi-sabi" did not exist "officially" before, it still exists.

Wabi-Sabi lives in discrete and overlooked details, the mirror and the skin, the litigation and the writing.

Over twenty years have gone since my original wabi-sabi formulations. Then the industrialised world began a significant effort to digitalise as much as possible of "reality" and translate it into "virtual" or "dematerialised" form. Then, a sense of "aesthetic realism" based on the nature of wabi-sab provided real comfort and inspiration to sensitive and creative souls. Does wabi-sab's essential analogue sensitivity still provide the emotional basis and the nourishment for the future? From a perspective and perhaps an idea, it can be helpful to look back at the time and place where the wabi tea party, wabi-sab's form and spirit took place.

Japan's Kyoto was involved in civilian crises during the sixteenth century. The mood of the population was calm, though not debilitating. Many valuable collections of sophisticated Chinese supplies have been destroyed. Such "perfect" products favour tea parties. Replacement facilities were needed. Japanese substitutes, albeit less refined and relatively crude, were reasonably priced and reasonably priced. Then they were used.

The location of this wabi / wabi-sabi invention was a tea room. Unlike previous luxury tea rooms, the wabi tea room was rustic and often housed in a small detached cottage, usually surrounded by a small garden.

In the beginning, what I call the "wabi era", the tea rooms were four and a half or about 81 square meters of the mat. At the end of the era, tea rooms can be 1/3 in size or 27 square meters. At the beginning of the Wabi era, participants of the ceremony came to their feet in the tea room. At the end of the episode, they began to crawl through a small opening in their hands and knees.

This compression of space, guided by artistic and "spiritual" motives, had the following effects:

* Temporary social status. (All participants were equally modest).

Closer human relations. (And the drama grew).

Remove all unnecessary items.

And by focusing more on what remains.

As the Wabi time advanced, lunch nooks and items became more straightforward and more modest. Improvisation has become an everyday habit. Purposes other than tea ceremonies are increasingly customised for use. For example, rice bowls were reused as tea films. Even broken and repaired items were used. The cause and effect have seen the consequences of use, abuse and accident.

It is clear from the above that the sensitivity, form and spirit of wabi-sab began primarily as an aesthetic adaptation to the catastrophic realities of the day.

There is parallelism in our time. Increasingly, we can distinguish the dark forms of the catastrophic scenarios ahead. The growing metropolitan population is projected to outstrip the catastrophically growing world population. How far do our material resources go? With damage repeatedly removed, are we forced to live in smaller and smaller environments with fewer and more modest objects?

It doesn't have to be tragic. Wabi-Sabi's beauty is based on modesty, even on the perceived poverty of elegance. The aesthetic pleasures of Wabi-Sab also depend on attitude and practice, or more than materiality itself. Subtlety and agility are at the heart of wabi-sab. Wabi-Sabi lives in marginalised and overlooked details, small and hidden, in litigation and the short term. But to appreciate these qualities, specific spiritual ways are needed: calmness, attention, and attention. If they are not present, wabi-sabi is invisible.

CHAPTER EIGHT

Design

Wabi-Sabi-design?

Through Wabi-Sab, it has recently become an interior trend, and philosophy itself has its roots in ancient Japanese culture. Broken, "wabi" refers to the atmosphere of unobtrusive rustic elegance or natural simplicity. At the same time, 'Sabi' is a feature of imperfection or seeing the beauty in the age-related errors. Together, wabi-sabi wants to look for authenticity and find joy in what things are instead of what they should be.

Let Wabi-Sabin look at home

Selling the total

Probably the best appearance of wabi-sabi is kintsugi art. Here the pottery is broken, and the pots were cast with gold or silver resin to replace the damage. Instead of hiding or replacing these songs, Kintsugi celebrates their age, fragility and history.

interior decoration inspiration architecture style furniture image source

From a design standpoint, it means accepting imperfection! Consider art furniture and craft supplies for your serial products. Handmade pieces may have minor flaws and points, but all this adds to their charm and character.

Principles in design

Wabi-Sabi is a Japanese way of thinking that has existed since the fifteenth century. It emerged in response to the prevailing trends of the time, which were mostly dependent on the decoration, scattering, and use of rare materials.

Directly wabi-sabi means finding beauty in imperfection. This involves connecting with a deep connection to the earth and enjoying the simple pleasures of life. First, it focuses on recognising the importance of authenticity and strives to remain genuine in all aspects of life.

For some, wabi-sabi is more of a guide than a design trend. It's about accepting things as they are, instead of wasting your time wanting something better and educating yourself to find the positive in less than ideal situations. While you are not prepared to do everything philosophically, incorporating some of these principles into your interior can be a good starting point.

Use natural materials

As much of the wabi sab is about to enter the country, and it is not surprising that this interior design is based on the use of natural materials. These materials can be incorporated regardless of their aesthetic preferences. For example, someone who favours Nordic design could build their plans around a light forest, while someone who enjoys the Mediterranean views may have a lot of terracotta.

No matter what material you use, authenticity is crucial. In this case, it is advisable to choose the right treatment for mass production forms. Consider a normal exit and buying interior design items from big stores. Flea markets, handicraft exhibitions and independently owned shops are viable alternatives.

Keep it simple

Once you have designed the design elements, it is essential to think about how to assemble all the pieces. With Wabi Sab, simplicity is a must. The original parts should allow themselves to shine and if possible, bring the element of nature into the room.

When it comes to doing these things, the best option is to focus on planning. The Wabi-Sabi interior fits in pairs with arrangements where the functional elements are the focus. Build a room around the furniture and make sure you leave a lot of negative space.

When you are ready to consider accessories, pay special attention to items that also have a functional purpose. Decorative bowls and a tray are always a solid option, as are houseplants that add freshness to space.

Take on the flaws

The last tip is the most important. Usually, when we talk about adding finishing touches to interior design, we talk about how to look finished or give it a professionally designed bit. In this case, you state the opposite.

Wabi-Sabi seeks the beauty of the existing flaws. With this in mind, feel free to leave the edges in the overall design. That decorative bowl that you hit again when it fell and cracked? You can name him a place of honour. Your messy bed? Here's permission to call it "cleverly messy."

Remember, however, that there is a difference between embracing the Wabi-Sabi essence and losing your design in your daily mess. Where this line falls is personal to each of us, but you want to make sure that aesthetic choices always have a purpose.

The Wabi-Sabi Materials

Unlike the present world, Wabi-Sabi does not seek perfection. Social networks have exacerbated the situation, while now people are comparing their looks, lives and achievements to Instagram tracking.

The word "wabi" means rustic simplicity and serenity, while "Sabi" means beauty and peace that comes with time and age.

This ancient Japanese philosophy based on Zen Buddhism encourages you to accept and enjoy life as it is: imperfect. The sooner you receive this, the sooner you will begin to appreciate the beauty of nature as a whole.

To create a Wabi-Sabi ambience at home, you need to add features such as old and handmade food, and a touch of natural materials to make your space comfortable. Not only that, but you are beginning to invest in durable and unique pieces. The Wabi-Sabi aspect cannot be achieved with manufactured machine elements, but it requires boats, natural ingredients and imperfect objects. The Wabi-Sabi aesthetic succeeds in worldly colours such as white or grey. Less is more: Objects must be chosen wisely.

Accepting Home History

Old houses have a unique character, and we think they should be maintained as much as possible. They are a legacy of past styles, people, lifestyles and history. It has the charm of a defective floor or noisy door. If you are renovating your basement, windows and furniture, leaving recesses and traces is a tribute to and preserves the soul of the home.

Make corrections with a gold leaf

You've probably heard of Japanese art in Kintsug, where broken dishes are decorated with gold, silver or platinum. The objective is to save the history of the object rather than hide it. This is perfect for the Wabi-Sab because it covers the shortcomings.

Antiques and antique furniture

Adding antique and antique furniture and accessories bring warmth and character to your room. You can also get some great songs on a budget and add a unique look to your home like this fantastic drugstore.

Fixed elements

The best 'non-existent' component in the room is the beautiful bouquet. The flowers are comfortable, inspiring and in the mood. By giving your home colour and numerous benefits, you can never go wrong.

Incomplete art

In artwork, sketches are perfect for incorporating Wabi-Sabi philosophy into your home. Usually, these are studies, researched ideas that do not seem complete or perfect but are more dynamic and open. The artist Richard Stark introduced here.

Concrete floors

Concrete floors are another great alternative to levels, as they also age with time. First, they have patches and cracks and are usually not perfect.

Handmade objects

Handmade items once again add a little soul to the home collection. Someone, personally do it, and it's probably a bit different from all the other songs, and that's why it's unique. Handmade ceramics are in vogue right now, and you can even make your dishes and create a beautiful table with your favourite recipes that add to the organic look of Wabi-Sab.

Antique Mirrors

Mirrors can add a touch of glamour to your space while staying true to the Wabi-Sabi look. They reflect light, illuminate the area and make it feel larger. The antique mirrors maintain the same aesthetics of the incomplete song that tells the story. If you already have a mirror for conversion, there are plenty of online guides that will teach you how to get to the old surface.

Natural materials

Raw materials like raw wood, stone or straw, as in the previous example, bring that natural energy into your home.

Textured walls

One of the critical features of Wabi-Sab is the patterned walls. It can be concrete, wood, brick or wallpaper with badly dying structures and barking parges.

CHAPTER NINE

Wabi-Sabi Art

Much of the Western world's belief in beauty originated in classical Greek art and was rooted in European ideals. Westerners see the beauty in the decay of the marble statue of Venus de Milo, in the majesty of the Sistine Chapel and the perfection of the anatomical drawings carefully represented by Leonardo Da Vinci. The Western battle is fighting for supremacy and burying the imperfections.

"The idea of wabi-sabi speaks of a willingness to accept things as they are. This goes against Western ideals that emphasise development and growth as essential parts of daily life. Requires the art of "slowness," a desire to focus on things that are often overlooked, shortcomings, and hints that depict time. "

The Western artistic idea drives artists to strive for perfection, to focus on advancement and self-development, and to prioritise finished products during the process. This encourages us to draw things "correctly" and accurately.

Place the Wabi-Sabi-tie

The Wabi-Sabi philosophy goes hand in hand with developing the artist's artistic style. After years of struggle and trying to get results with my art, I began to study, play and experiment with my sketches. I wanted to be released, and I let the process go under control. First, I stopped drawing with a pen, carefully planned the song in detail, and began to let my hand guide me. I made many incredible drawings that were full of mistakes and failures.

But I opened up, accepted where I was on the artistic journey, and learned to see my art as it is, not as I want it to be.

"Wabi-Sabi values all authenticity by recognising three simple realities: nothing lasts, nothing is complete, and nothing is perfect."

And slowly, my "mistakes" began to take me on new and different paths. I started experimenting with drawing methods I had never tried, tools I had never used, and began to develop a freer and more playful mindset while drawing.

Creating art in this way does not mean mistakes. There is no wrong way to make your art. Participating in this philosophy freed me from the anxiety and anxiety that prevented me from knowing the art of making and sometimes preventing me from making art.

"Nothing is a mistake. There is no gain or failure; there is only.

Making art in a Wabi-Sabi way allows us to be more present in the process, leaving tools and materials part of the art. It is about making the process more important than a finished work of art. It is not about trying to force a particular result.

Wabi-Sabi does not tell us what our artistic style is or where we are going. It tells us to appreciate and see the beauty of where we are now. This tells us that we are not obsessed with the future when our art is "better", or we focus on the day when we are finally "successful". Instead, we should appreciate where we are on the road today and enjoy the art we produce today.

There is no ambition, laziness or renunciation of learning in this mental state.

It is acceptance and comfort on the way, patience in the process and appreciation for the present.

My philosophy on Wabi-Sabi art

This is a brief manifestation of how I think the Wabi-Sabi mentality can be used to create art.
Nourish the process, not the end product.

Learn to love the process of creating art and discovering our artistic styles. Making is the most important thing, not the last work of art. Art is permanent, but what we learn about making art lasts forever.

Be patient and believe modestly.

Forget the illusions of honour, success and prosperity. Reduce our search to "meet" or "become great artists" and learn to love and appreciate our art as such instead of continually trying to supplement it.

Observe and embrace the shortcomings of art.

Be aware and understand what comes naturally to us. Accept yourself and value yourself as the artists we are today, including flaws and mistakes.

We appreciate where we are and enjoy the trip.

Don't focus on the future. The value of where we are today is meant to be explored and the best we can, but we value where we are today.

Follow our intuition about other people's rules and artistic ideals.

Develop a deep understanding of yourself and be compassionate about yourself and the arts. Let our hands guide us, and what we are told is not the "right" way to create art. A return from formula-based rational drawing to a more natural and intuitive art form.

Take advantage of yourself and see a sketch of beauty.

Celebrate our sketchbooks and embrace transition work, ongoing and unfinished inside. Our sketches are always in a state of change, continually evolving, and are never perfect, just like us and our art.

Developing the Wabi-Sabi spirit

This way of wabi-sabi and practising, our artistic styles are life's journey. Wrong wabi-sabi, we will only find your artistic style through experience, deep understanding of ourselves and the passage of time. The more we can be aware of and appreciate ourselves, the more authenticity and authenticity we have in our works of art.

Creating art in the Wabi-Sabi way ultimately means learning how to investigate our masterful styles, appreciate where we are today on our imaginative adventures, accept mistakes and rely on the process.

The embrace of imperfection and the continuous development of our art relieve us of the many anxieties that prevent us from making art that feels our part or making art at all.

This way of staying calm with our artists and making friends with our art comes only to us through the artistic creation process.

We can get ourselves and our art by working.

"Bottles and tangled hair, with bent knees and cracking of the lips. This morning, I am incomplete and alive. It will be a new bath!"

The art of imperfection

With new ties to Chinese Buddhism, Wabi-Sabi flourished during Japanese tea ceremonies in the 15th and 16th centuries. "Wabi-Sabi is a difficult concept, so it's hard to define in a few words," Adams says. "It's the beauty that is celebrated in a lasting, imperfect and imperfect way. Wabi means living in a simple way and harmony with nature, combining things with the essentials so you can appreciate them even more; I knew, spent and spent time.".

Always prevalent in the modern world, where Instagram is constantly promoting perfectionism and millennials are exhausted, wabi-sabi offers the opposite. For Adams, the concept is "the antidote to all great perfection." It provides the ability to reduce speed and appreciate the moments in life when we tend to be "24/7".

"It means living in a way that attracts attention and values the beauty of everyday life," Adams says.

And just as Sunday's Edit encourages you to embrace positivity in your image, the wabi-sabi app can be used to accept home faults in a safe space. In 2018, Etsy Trend Guide predicted wabi sab is a growing trend in interior design. And the pace just increased.

"Interior design is currently inspiring the natural world, and we bring the beauty of nature inside," says Homepolish designer Amy Row. "Textured Terracotta Tiles, Large Trees such as House Plants, Plastered Walls, Furniture Raw Materials such as Blended Wood and Concrete."

With this in mind, Adams and Row have some suggestions on how to incorporate wabi-sabi aesthetics into your home.

Take advantage of beauty and usefulness.

"It covers beauty with something useful, like looking for a nice storage basket, a good barrel of table water, or even a beautifully designed toilet brush; it's small things," Adams says.

But wabi-sabi does not mean decoration without a careful examination of the details. "At first, it's easy to convince yourself that finding wabi-sab means uninvited and unfortunately, stylish elements. Instead, you have to look for elements that have soul and character in themselves," he says.

Add a personal touch

Photos you recently discarded? Get them out. "Customize your home by including items that are likely to be only valuable to you: family photos, souvenirs, children's art, etc.

Make it happen

Looking for more specific forms of "wabi-sabi" for your home? "Create your dining tables using a coarse stone edge plate directly from the stone importer. The stone importers' stone tiles are made and cut to desired dimensions, but labour is often more expensive than the stone itself," Row says. I found a local concrete storage platform for the specific platform, and you can place a stone with the edges just above it. "

In terms of wall features, Row loves Calico Wallpaper's Satori collection, which was inspired by Kintsugi (Japanese Traditional Ceramics) when she fell in love with a wabi sab from the Satori collection. The second option? "Place the tile in the base and do not use spacers or mortar.

Made in the USA
Coppell, TX
11 January 2020

14347534R10118